KNOWLEDGE AND EXPERIENCE

KNOWLEDGE
AND
EXPERIENCE

Proceedings
of the
1962 Oberlin Colloquium
in Philosophy

Edited
by
C. D. Rollins

UNIVERSITY OF PITTSBURGH PRESS

Second Printing, 1966

PREFACE

The papers in this volume are the outcome of the third annual Oberlin Colloquium held April 20-22, 1962, at Oberlin College under the auspices of the Department of Philosophy. As the contents of the volume make evident it was possible, in arranging the 1962 Colloquium, to call five sessions without departing from our policy that no two sessions should be concurrent and that each should permit as much question and answer as might be desired.

It will be seen that the papers deal with two overlapping topics, knowledge and experience, and that the authors pursue a type of philosophical inquiry commonly called "analytic." While philosophy of this type has had a long history, today it owes much to recent British philosophers. It happens that several of the sessions here presented are concerned particularly with the work of a Cambridge philosopher and with that of an Oxford one—the late Ludwig Wittgenstein and the late John L. Austin.

The opening paper by Mr. Warnock deals with Austin's "purified version" of the correspondence theory of truth—a version employing the notions of both demonstrative conventions and descriptive conventions. Warnock examines a number of objections, chiefly by Strawson, and concludes that in this version the theory is by no means so faulty as it has been taken to be.

Next, Mr. Prior turns to the *Sophismata* of the fourteenth-century writer John Buridan for three puzzles of self-reference. Two of them, employing the concepts of knowledge and doubt, are developed and analyzed in some detail. Prior then sketches a formal language, in the Lukasiewicz notation, which can be useful in representing such paradoxes; but he notes that it cannot be extended to include its own semantics.

In the first symposium Mr. Searle investigates recent attempts like those of Hare and Strawson to analyze the meanings of certain words in terms of performances, that is to say in terms of the kinds of speech acts which are commonly performed in the utterance of those words. He considers such philosophically troubling words as 'true' and 'good,' and examines the thesis that a speech-act analysis does not merely tell us about the acts performed in the uttering, but actually gives or analyzes the meanings, or parts of the meanings, of those words. Whether we suppose the speech acts actually to be performed or merely to be "in the offing," he argues, the thesis is plainly discredited by examples; for there are sentences of various kinds (e.g. hypotheticals) wherein the words in question occur with their literal meanings while yet those meanings are not associated with the alleged sorts of speech act. Searle goes on to diagnose the mistake as stemming from a misinterpretation of the theory that the meaning of a word is its use, combined with an exclusive concentration on one kind of sentence, the simple indicative. In the final section of the paper, he considers what positive contribution toward conceptual analysis may be ascribed to the thesis he rejects. In his comments on Searle, Mr. Vendler holds that the correct view of speech acts and meanings lies somewhere between the one Searle rejects and Searle's own; and he proposes a guide for determining the meaning of a word in another way. Mr. Benacerraf, believing that Searle is attacking a view seldom held and that the attack is inconclusive, indicates some features of a type of meaning analysis he himself would prefer, one which he takes to be compatible with Searle's approach.

Exactly what are "criteria" as Wittgenstein speaks of them in his later work? Mr. Garver finds thirteen features which characterize them, and he notes wherein he diverges from the conclusions of other students of the same texts. Among objections by the commentators, two are perhaps the most emphatic: Mr. Ginet maintains that Garver's account does not properly indicate the relations between criteria for, and conditions that are necessary and sufficient for, the application of a word or expression; and Mr. Siegler suggests, while Mr. Ziff argues, that Wittgenstein had no logical theory at all. Garver's concessions, in rejoining, extend to neither of these points.

In the final symposium Mr. Castañeda takes issue with Wittgenstein and Malcolm and others. He defends, against what he sees as an attempted *reductio ad absurdum*, the logical possibility of a language that is inherently private. He uses the principle that a private language cannot, as language, be required to pass tests which even a public language could not pass, nor to pass tests which only public languages could by definition pass. He then rejects familiar Wittgensteinian arguments from the contingency of psychological ascriptions, from "point" and "question," from the nature of rule-following, and from the possibility of mistakes and corrections. Against this Mr. Chappell, while granting that "the" private-language argument is unclear, objects that Wittgenstein and Malcolm did not conceive a private language in the way Castañeda does, and that the proposed *reductio* is not maintained by either of them; further, that in any case Castañeda, in assuming some syntax for a private language, has begged the real question, and has failed to show that in a private language there can be rules or any question of correctness or of error. Mr. Thomson, also doubtful that

Wittgenstein held just what Castañeda takes him to have held, suggests that Castañeda is at cross purposes with both Wittgenstein and Malcolm, and views the private-language issue as being too unclear for judgment to be passed upon it. In his rejoinders, Castañeda shows himself in agreement more with Thomson than with Chappell.

In the symposia, of course, each main paper is to be taken as opening up discussion and leading to replies and rejoinders. Where a commentator's remarks have grown nearly to the length of the main paper, it will be evident that the commentary as it now stands is an expansion of the original version. In fact not one of the papers in the volume now reads throughout exactly as it was delivered.

Only one paper, the main one by Mr. Searle, has appeared elsewhere in print. It was the leading article in the *Philosophical Review* for October, 1962, and we thank the editors of the *Review* for permission to reprint it. Yet as the paper appears here, it contains a number of altered passages, and two considerable additions, one of them at the end. It should also be noted that a longer and augmented version of the main paper by Mr. Castañeda was circulated before the meetings, as were abstracts of main papers for all three symposia.

While visitors at the meetings represented approximately twenty universities and colleges in this country and abroad, the speakers came from twelve: Mr. Warnock from Oxford and Princeton, Mr. Prior from Manchester and Chicago, Mr. Searle from Michigan and California (Berkeley), Mr. Vendler from Cornell, Mr. Benacerraf from Princeton, Mr. Garver from Buffalo, Mr. Ginet from Ohio State University, Mr. Siegler from Chicago, Mr. Ziff from Pennsylvania, Mr. Castañeda from Wayne State University, Mr. Chappell from Chicago, and Mr. Thomson from Oxford (Corpus Christi) and Columbia.

Members of the Oberlin faculty in philosophy are indebted to the contributors for their generous cooperation, and grateful to visitors generally for an occasion made both pleasant and fruitful. We hope that the publication of these proceedings may contribute in some measure to the resolution of the issues under discussion and may also help to encourage meetings which put aside all else for the give-and-take of intent philosophical inquiry.

C.D.R.

The editor acknowledges that preparation of this volume was facilitated by the tenure of an Andrew Mellon Postdoctoral Fellowship in Philosophy at the University of Pittsburgh during leave from Oberlin College.

CONTENTS

TRUTH AND CORRESPONDENCE. 11
    G. J. Warnock

SOME EXERCISES IN EPISTEMIC LOGIC. . . . 21
    A. N. Prior

Symposium

MEANING AND SPEECH ACTS 28
    John R. Searle

COMMENTS 38
    Zeno Vendler

COMMENTS 43
    Paul Benacerraf

REJOINDERS 50
    John R. Searle

Symposium

WITTGENSTEIN ON CRITERIA 55
    Newton Garver

COMMENTS 72
    Carl Ginet

COMMENTS 77
    F. A. Siegler

CONTENTS

COMMENTS 81
    Paul Ziff

REJOINDERS 86
    Newton Garver

Symposium

THE PRIVATE-LANGUAGE ARGUMENT 88
    H-N. Castañeda

COMMENTS 106
    V. C. Chappell

COMMENTS 119
    J. F. Thomson

REJOINDERS 125
    H-N. Castañeda

TRUTH AND CORRESPONDENCE

G. J. WARNOCK

1. As philosophical theories go, the so-called Correspondence Theory of Truth has had a pretty long life, and I hope I am not alone in thinking that it is not dead yet. It has, indeed, quite recently been pronounced dead. In 1950 the late J. L. Austin propounded what has been called a "purified version" of the theory, in reply to which Mr. P. F. Strawson contended—with, I think it has been widely supposed, conclusive success—that the theory could not be purified: it needed to be interred.[1] However, it is not clear to me that Mr. Strawson's grounds for saying this were conclusive; so that the Correspondence Theory is not yet, in my view, a plainly dead duck. In this paper I shall consider some of the objections which have been or which might be urged against it.

Austin's "purified version" runs briefly as follows. Let us take it, he says, that it is statements which primarily or centrally are said to be true or untrue. It is then, he thinks, correct to say—so correct indeed as to be somewhat platitudinous—that a statement's being true consists in its "correspondence" to something "in the world"— the expression 'the world' here being used to designate quite generally the subject-matter of possible statement-making discourse. Where purification is called for is not, he thinks, in saying this much, but only in going on to give an account of what is to be understood here by the term 'correspondence.' What is it for a statement to "correspond to" something in the world?

To this question Austin offers an answer in two stages. Consider for example the words 'The corn is green.' There are in the first place, Austin says, "descriptive conventions" by which these words are "correlated" with a certain *type* of situation, or state of affairs, to be found (perhaps) in the world; and, roughly speaking, to know what these conventions are is to know what the English sentence

[1] See Symposium on Truth, Aristotelian Society Supplementary Volume XXIV, 1950, pp. 111–172; also J. L. Austin, *Philosophical Papers*, Oxford, 1961, pp. 85–101. Perhaps I should mention here that the present paper examines some points not examined in another (not yet published) paper dealing with the same cluster of issues: in particular I consider there, and do not consider here, the question whether it is, as Mr. Strawson has argued, mistaken in principle to suppose that one who says that what someone has said is true thereby makes a statement about a statement, or a further assertion about an assertion, or says something about what the (other) speaker has said. I believe, for reasons too lengthy to be rehearsed here, that this very natural supposition is not mistaken. But besides this there are, of course, many other issues of interest, importance, and relevance not touched on in the pages that follow.

'The corn is green' means. But second, there are also "demonstrative conventions" correlating, not the words but particular utterances of the words, with particular—in Austin's term "historic"—situations or states of affairs to be found at particular times or places in the world; and to know what these conventions are is to be in a position to know (given the context of utterance) what *particular* state of affairs one who says on some occasion that the corn is green, is alluding to. The statement that the corn is green is said to be true, then, when it corresponds to something in the world in the following sense: the words 'The corn is green,' as uttered on some particular occasion, are correlated by the demonstrative conventions with a historic situation or state of affairs which is of the type with which, in the language, the words 'The corn is green' are correlated by the descriptive conventions.[2]

2. Now this account of the matter, which Austin evidently regarded as rather obviously correct, has in fact been objected to on a good many grounds. Let us first take this one. Austin's account, it might be said, offers to elucidate the notion of truth in terms of the correspondence of statements to something "in the world"; but it does not actually do this. If we consider the statement that the corn is green, we see that there is indeed something in the world to which the words 'the corn' could (not very felicitously) be said to correspond —namely, that corn which the speaker refers to, which his statement is about. But there is actually nothing at all in the world with which the statement *as a whole* could be said to correspond, in the way in which the referring expression 'the corn' could be said to correspond to the corn. To put it rather roughly: only objects (such as corn) are genuinely in the world; those entities, "situations" or "states of affairs," to which in Austin's account true statements are said to correspond are plainly not, however, objects, and hence are not in the world.

Now this objection aims, it may be, at a serious point; but there is surely not very much in what it actually says. For it is surely both quite good sense and perfectly good English to speak, say, of the political situation in Cuba in 1959, or of the state of affairs in my cornfield at the end of May 1962; and do we not here have places and dates used, quite naturally, to identify particular situations or states of affairs? How could this be done, if they were not in any sense at all in space or time? A state of affairs, no doubt, is not an object, and does not have a neatly bounded place in the world *just as* an object typically does; but is this the only sense in which anything can be said to be in the world? Suppose I were to say that one-party dictatorships are sometimes very popular; would it not be

[2] See J. L. Austin, *Philosophical Papers*, p. 90.

quite proper for a sceptical interlocutor to ask where in the world such a state of affairs is to be found? And might I not answer quite properly, even truly perhaps, "In Cuba, for instance"? There does not appear to me to be any better reason for denying that situations, say, can be in the world than there would be for denying that reflections, say, can be in mirrors. The expression 'the situation in Cuba' is not indeed exactly analogous with the expression 'the house in Cuba,' just as the expression 'the reflection in the mirror' is not exactly analogous with the expression 'the glass in the mirror.' But what this seems to show is only that 'in' has somewhat different uses.

3. It might more seriously be objected, however, that to look, as Austin does, for something "in the world" to which a true statement as a whole can be said to correspond is inevitably to reduce one's account of truth to triviality, to the status of a wholly unilluminating *pseudo*-account. The most natural candidate, so Mr. Strawson has argued, for the role of that in the world to which a true statement corresponds is "a fact." But to say that a true statement corresponds to a fact is to say practically nothing; for there is no way of identifying a fact except as that which some true statement states; so that to say that a true statement corresponds to a fact is in effect to produce the markedly unenlivening tautology that a true statement states what that statement, if it is true, does state.

This objection, however, is not as it stands strictly applicable to what Austin says. For his account of truth does not employ the term 'fact'; it employs the terms 'situation' and 'state of affairs.' Does this difference matter? I am inclined to think, though with some trepidation and uncertainty, that it does.

I take it that the nerve of the objection to the use, in this context, of the expression 'fact' is that, in Mr. Strawson's words, 'fact' is wedded to 'that'-clauses.[3] The fact with which, if with any, the statement that the corn is green is correlated is the fact that the corn is green; but this fact is simply what the statement states, or what one who makes that statement alleges. The fact that the corn is green does not "make" the statement that the corn is green true or untrue; for, on the one hand, if the statement is not true, there is no such fact; while, on the other hand, if the statement is true, then that there is such a fact is quite trivially analytic. As we expressed it a moment ago, there is no way of identifying a fact except as that which some true statement states, or as that which some person states in making a true statement; so that here we have absolutely no explanatory leverage.

[3] It should be noted that Austin had questions to raise about this. See *Philosophical Papers*, pp. 102–122.

But the case is surely otherwise with states of affairs. If I hear someone say that the corn is green, then certainly, if I understand his words, I know what sort or "type" of state of affairs he is alleging to obtain; but there also arises the further question, what *particular* state of affairs his utterance alludes to. Well, I learn, let us say, that he is alluding to the state of affairs currently obtaining in my hundred-acre field. So far, so good; but it does not of course follow from any of this that what he says is true, or again untrue. To determine that question I may need to go to my hundred-acre field and examine the state of affairs there obtaining; and what I observe there may "make" what he says true—or, of course, it may not. Whereas, one might say, a statement is related to a fact not at all if it is false, and trivially if it is true, it may be related to, "correlated" with, a particular state of affairs and be in fact *either* true *or* false *of* that state of affairs; and the "type" of that state of affairs is what "makes" it true or false. I do not see in this either an impropriety, or a triviality. To put it succinctly, Austin's account embodies, what doubtless talk of "correspondence with facts" undesirably obscures, the distinction between meaning ("descriptive conventions") and reference ("demonstrative conventions"); and I cannot suppose that anyone would wish to hold either that this distinction is not important, or that it is not of central relevance to the question what it is for a statement to be true.

Again, it has been said that facts are "*quasi*-linguistic" entities, and for that reason unsuited to illuminate the nature of truth; but, if I know what this means, it would seem that the same thing is *not* true of situations. Facts, I suppose, might be said to be "linguistic" for such reasons as these: people *state* facts, much as they state (say) propositions; facts are, much as (say) statements are, very often *about* things; we refer to a fact, as we refer to what someone said, with a 'that'-clause. The fact that there are tigers in India is a fact about the fauna of India, and is what someone states who says truly that there are tigers there. But situations are not, like facts, stated; they may be, like tables, described. They cannot, as facts can, be said to be "about" anything. The expression 'the situation that . . .' is not admissible English. It appears, then, that if the term 'fact' is objectionable in this connection, it at least cannot be for just the same reasons that the terms 'situation' and 'state of affairs' are objectionable; a new case, if there is one, would need to be made out against them.

4. But, it may next be urged, though the distinction between meaning and reference is doubtless of importance, Austin's mode of stating and employing it is nevertheless infelicitous. There fall, I think, to be considered here two objections—objections which, if I am right, rather neatly cancel each other out.

(i) What would we ordinarily say that a statement, or one who utters a statement, refers to? To what the statement is about. What then is the statement that the corn is green about? Surely it is about the corn—in particular, let us suppose, about the corn now standing in my hundred-acre field. All this seems very clear: and would it not be vastly preferable to state the matter in this way, rather than to nominate, as Austin does, so relatively perplexing an entity as the *state of affairs* in my hundred-acre field as that with which the statement is "demonstratively correlated"? The expressions 'situation' and 'state of affairs' are certainly vague and perhaps obscure in significance; situations and states of affairs are somewhat abstract entities; and what reason is there for bringing them in at this point, rather than such familiar objects as corn, cats, cabbages, and kings —the *things* in the world that from time to time we refer to, or talk about? We do, indeed, sometimes refer to situations, as in 'The situation in my hundred-acre field is deteriorating daily'; but should not this very special case be distinguished from that of such earthier, less abstract locutions as 'The corn is green'?

I think, however, that it is not difficult to see a reason for Austin's choice of terminology at this point. It seems perfectly proper to say in general, though admittedly in somewhat distressingly abstract terms, that one who makes a statement thereby says that some state of affairs obtains, and that whether or not his statement is true is a matter of whether or not the particular state of affairs he alludes to is of the character, kind, or type of which, in his utterance, he says that it is. It is, by contrast, plainly not possible to say in general, even though the terms be less alarmingly abstract, that one who makes a statement thereby says something about some thing or things to which he refers; for this is true, of course, only of statements of a certain sort, namely, those which do happen to be about, or to refer to, some particular thing or things. If I say, for instance, that there are no green dogs, I allude presumably to the present state of affairs in the animal kingdom; but I do not refer to green dogs, nor to any other dogs, or animals, or even objects. Thus, while the terminology of 'situations' and 'states of affairs' may justly be thought to have the demerit of abstractness, and even of some measure of obscurity, it may be held to have the compensating virtue, for the present purpose, of general applicability.

(ii) Consideration of this latter objection disposes also, I believe, of the next one. It has been urged by Mr. Strawson against Austin's account that it is, among other things, undesirably narrow in its range of application; by implying, as Austin does, that all stating involves both "demonstration" and "description," does he not implicitly restrict his account to that particular variety of stating which does consist in saying something about some particular thing or things? Does it not appear that he has overlooked the existence of statements in which nothing (in particular) is referred to, no object is talked about?

But it will be evident, I think, that there is a misunderstanding here. For, as we have just seen, Austin's words are so chosen as precisely to avoid the restrictiveness with which he is thus charged. Mr. Strawson evidently took Austin to be claiming, or perhaps to be inadvertently implying, that every statement must involve demonstrative conventions in the sense that it must refer to, or be about, some individual thing (object, event, etc.) or things, as 'The cat is white' refers to or is about this particular cat. This would indeed be pretty intolerably restrictive; and it would indeed be pertinent to object to this claim, or this implication, that 'There are white cats' is an evident counter-example, since of course in making the statement that there are white cats I do not allude to any white cats in particular, and could not properly be asked *which* white cats I am saying that there are. But the fact is that Austin's account does not actually have the implication which Mr. Strawson claims to find in it. For that with which a statement is, in Austin's sense, correlated by demonstrative conventions is never a particular thing or things—not, for instance, a particular cat; but rather a particular situation or state of affairs—for instance, the particular situation of some cat's being (or possibly not being) white. It is plain that this is a substantially different matter; for one thing, it is plain that two or more statements about a cat might all refer, in Mr. Strawson's sense, to the same thing, namely the same cat, while being demonstratively correlated, in Austin's sense, with quite different things, namely two or more different states of affairs in the presumably quite varied life-history of the cat.

5. In saying, then, or implying that all stating involves both demonstrative and descriptive conventions, Austin is not espousing the certainly most restrictive and unappealing doctrine that all statements must be about, must refer to, some individual thing or things. However, the question does of course still arise whether or not, when we have cleared this misunderstanding out of the way, it is actually correct to imply, as he does, that "demonstrative conventions" are involved in the making of *any* true statement. There remain, I think, serious grounds on which this might be questioned.

Let us ask, then, this question: what does Austin's assumption of the general necessity of both demonstrative and descriptive conventions presuppose? What would have to be the case for it to be true? Well, what his view presupposes, I believe, is this: that any statement is such that (i) it is possible for states of affairs in the world either to be or not be of the "type" which it asserts to obtain; and also such that (ii) we might, at least in principle, come across states of affairs whose being of that type would not establish its truth, and whose not being of that type would not establish its falsehood. For in the case of any statement satisfying these conditions, since there will be in the world states of affairs not *relevant* to its truth or falsehood, the question whether it is true or false must raise the prior question what particular state of affairs is being alluded to, and thus may relevantly be investigated; and to answer this question we must make use of demonstrative conventions. For example: cats may in general be either white or not white; and further, when I state on some particular occasion that the cat is white, there will be some cats whose whiteness does not establish that my statement is true, and some cats whose tabbiness, say, does not establish that it is false. Thus, if we are to consider profitably whether or not my statement that the cat is white is true, we need to be apprised, by way of the appropriate demonstrative conventions, what particular state of affairs—roughly, which cat when—it would be to the point for us to take a look at.

The question now arises, then, whether it can be held that statements in general must satisfy the above two conditions. Well, I think this much at any rate can be said: that any statement must satisfy these conditions, *if* we are ever to be in a position to pronounce it to be true on empirical grounds. It is fairly obvious, I think, that this is so. For if we are to be in a position to pronounce statements to be true on empirical grounds, we must do so by investigation of the appropriate states of affairs in the world; but, however many such states of affairs we might investigate, it seems reasonable to suppose that there would always be indefinitely many that we have not investigated; and thus, if our investigations are ever to reach a point at which we are entitled to pronounce our statements to be true, it appears that we must be entitled, at some point, to hold as not relevant the indefinitely many further states of affairs which we have not investigated. But, if we are to do this, we must of course be in a position to say that a statement relates to *this* state, or *these* states, of affairs and *not* to others; and to be in a position to say this is to rely on "demonstrative conventions" in Austin's sense.

6. Thus Austin's "purified version" of the Correspondence Theory is not, in my submission, grossly and intolerably restricted in its range of application in the way that Mr. Strawson has suggested—restricted, that is, roughly speaking to the special case of subject-predicate statements about individual things. The restriction actually implied by its incorporation into his account of truth of *both* demonstrative *and* descriptive conventions is, rather, that his account fits the case only of utterances which, in principle at least, we could be in a position to pronounce to be true on empirical grounds. But here a rather important question very naturally arises which, I regret

B

to say, I have no notion how to answer. I can set up the pieces, so to speak, but I don't know what moves to make, and am not doing much more, in the rest of this paper, than appealing for help.

The difficulty is this. One may, I think, very naturally feel that Austin's account, even if not too narrow in the extreme way that Mr. Strawson suggests, is nevertheless too narrow; for surely there are a good many kinds of utterances to which his account has at least no obvious or natural application, but which are yet, very often and very naturally, said to be true. There are, first of all, analytic statements, or theorems in logic, or in mathematics; these of course are not asserted on empirical grounds, and there is no question here of our needing to know which "states of affairs in the world" would be relevant to their truth or falsity, since none would be so relevant; but surely we do often apply to them the predicate 'true.' Then too, what about the case of quite general statements of natural law? If I say, for instance, that metals expand when heated, I do not mean, and would not be taken to mean, that this state of affairs obtains in some particular part or parts of the world, or over certain particular stretches of the world's history; there can be no place, surely, for "demonstrative conventions" here, since my statement is of unrestricted generality; but can it not be said to be *true* that metals expand when heated?

Now, in defence of Austin's account against this objection, it might conceivably be argued that the cases here brought up, which his account of truth certainly does not appear to cater for, are not counter-examples since they are not examples of truths. An analytic proposition, it might be argued, is not true or false, but either necessary or impossible; a well-proved proposition in logic or in mathematics is not true but valid, not a truth but a theorem: that metals expand when heated can be said to be strongly confirmed, to be much-tested and not falsified, but not to be true. Yet it will probably be felt, and with some reason, that to take this line would be somewhat high-handed. After all we do speak often enough of necessary truth, or of truths of logic; and if we accept some well-confirmed statement of natural law, we find it entirely natural to say that it is true. It might possibly be argued that these ways of speaking are in some ways undesirable, undiscriminating, potentially misleading, or whatnot; but on what grounds could it be declared that to speak as we thus do is flatly wrong?

The next defensive move, then, which suggests itself is to hold that, although it is perfectly permissible or proper to apply the predicate 'true' to, for instance, theorems in logic or formulations of natural law, the "sense" of the word in such applications is different, or even, more ambitiously perhaps, that its meaning is different. I am inclined to think, though I am by no means sure, that Austin would have said this. At any rate the view underlying, and probably indeed required for the tenability of, his account of truth seems to be that there is what might be called a central or primary use of 'true'—namely its use in application to utterances made, and pronounced to be true or false, on empirical grounds, in the light of the relevant states of affairs in the world; that the (purified) Correspondence Theory of truth quite rightly concentrates on, and characterizes in a general way, this central use; but that the word 'true' may also be used in other contexts than these, in "senses" more or less different and remote from its central or primary meaning, and calling for elucidation in more or less different terms.[4]

As to the merits of this view, however, I feel both very uncertain, and regrettably helpless. On the one hand, there seems a good deal to be said for the view that 'true,' like 'good,' should not be represented as having different senses, or meanings, in its different occurrences; though of course the grounds on which, or criteria by which, it is applied must be admitted to be different, and indeed of different kinds, in different cases. If so, it would follow that a general account of what 'true' means ought to fit the cases equally of, for instance, contingent and necessary truths. But on the other hand, one may feel that the analogy with 'good' is perhaps not a sound one here—that the shift from contingent to necessary truth is greater than, or somehow different in character from, the shifts from, say, evaluating apples to evaluating arguments, and is in fact radical enough to justify our speaking of a shift to another "sense." But perhaps my uncertainty about which way to go here is simply evidence of the fact that I have not—has anybody?—a theory about "senses" of words in the light of which such an uncertainty could be resolved. Without a doctrine, perhaps, one can do nothing here but fumble around, more or less persuasively but still inconclusively.

At the moment, at any rate, I think I cannot do more than propose that this question in particular needs further investigation. If it were decided that 'true' in all its uses, or at least in all its uses in application to things written or said or otherwise uttered, is to be

[4] What Austin says in his paper is carefully guarded on this point, indeed deliberately non-committal. "When is a statement not a statement? When it is a formula in a calculus: when it is a performative utterance: when it is a value-judgment: when it is a definition: when it is part of a work of fiction. . . . It is a matter for decision how far we should continue to call such masqueraders 'statements' at all, and how widely we should be prepared to extend the uses of 'true' and 'false' in 'different senses'. My own feeling is that it is better, when once a masquerader has been unmasked, *not* to call it a statement and *not* to say it is true or false." See *Philosophical Papers*, p. 99. But this position, carefully guarded though it is, seems doubtfully tenable; for it seems to have been decided already, *omnium consensu*, that, for instance, theorems in a calculus may be said to be true; and it is not clear to me how, even if we withold from them the appellation of "statements", they could be held only to "masquerade" as truths. I believe, then, that Austin would have been obliged, in some cases at least, to countenance what he envisages as an "extension" of the uses of 'true' and 'false', in "different senses".

regarded as strictly univocal, then it would follow that the Correspondence Theory of Truth, even in Austin's (and perhaps in any other) "purified version," is too restricted, and so not acceptable as a general account of truth. But if we allow ourselves the luxury of different "senses," then the Correspondence Theory has, so far as I can see, a still undefeated claim to be considered a sound account, so far as it goes, of the central sense, or of one of the more central senses. I should have liked to come to some more definite or more ambitious conclusion than this, but have not, I fear, been able to see my way to doing so. I do not at present see how we are to decide whether, in for instance the sentences 'It's true that he is bald' and 'That a triangle has three sides is true,' the word 'true' should or should not be said to have different senses. I should be glad to be told.

SOME EXERCISES IN EPISTEMIC LOGIC

A. N. PRIOR

I propose to consider one or two puzzles from the eighth chapter of John Buridan's *Sophismata*. Buridan's popular fame rests on the story attributed to him of a donkey which had before it two equally distant and equally attractive piles of hay, one on each side of it, and which starved for lack of a sufficient reason either to turn to the right or to the left. I do not know where this story occurs in Buridan's works, or even whether it occurs there at all, but it is true that he had an eye for picturesque illustrations. One of his favorite doctrines was that a proposition occurring as a subordinate clause does not there occur as a proposition at all, and is quite a different sort of thing from what it is when it occurs on its own. (I think Ryle has propounded a similar doctrine in " 'If,' 'So' and 'Because' "). Buridan gives the example of the Psalmist's proposition that 'The fool hath said in his heart, There is no God.' That David was inspired to write this sentence, does not at all entail that he was inspired to write the false and impious sentence, 'There is no God.' As it occurs in the psalm, Buridan says, this is no more a sentence than a part of a worm is a worm, though a part of a worm will become a worm if you chop the worm in two.

The donkey story—which has possibly led to a widespread popular confusion between Buridan and Balaam—is supposed to have something to do with free will, but it could well come up in a logical context, and Mr. C. A. Meredith of Dublin has described as "Buridanian" those propositions which, like 'What I am now saying is true,' are not exactly paradoxical, since they do not lead to contradictions, but are essentially undecidable. Meredith recommended simply counting all such propositions as true—they do no harm. If we object to the idea of making propositions true or false by our free choice in this way, we could perhaps point to such propositions as showing that truth is wider than knowledge—they must be either true or false, but there is no possible way in which anyone could find out which they are.

Buridan was in fact interested in propositions of this sort, and constructed examples for which Meredith's solution just would not work at all. Suppose, for example, that Socrates says, 'What Plato says is false,' and says nothing else, and Plato says, 'What Socrates says is false,' and says nothing else. One thing which seems clear about these propositions is that they must have different truth-values—if either of them is true, the other is false, and if either is false, the other is true. Oddly enough, however, this is one thing about them which Buridan does not accept—he introduces a principle of equity, by which he argues that they *must* have the same truth-value, because any argument for or against either of them can be matched by an exactly parallel argument for or against the other. And having laid this down, he bangs their quarrelsome heads together and decrees that they are both false. It can be argued, he admits, that if what Plato says is also false, then what Socrates says cannot be false, because he says precisely *that* what Plato says is false, and *ex hypothesi* this is how things actually are. Buridan, in answer to this, admits that things are as Socrates says they are, but says that in circumstances like this even propositions which formally accord with the facts may be false because, taken together with the circumstances, they lead to a contradiction, namely to the conclusion that they are themselves at once true, because things are as they say they are, and false, because of this principle of equity.

Buridan then considers a further objection, and a very ingenious one at that. Suppose, he says, that a third party named Robert turns up, and says exactly what Socrates says, namely that what Plato says is false. Won't *he* at least be right, since *ex hypothesi* what Plato says *is* false? And yet we can suppose Socrates and Robert not merely to say the same thing but to say it for the same reason, namely that both of them are somehow under the impression that what Plato has said is, 'There is no God.' The point of introducing this little error is plain. No man in his senses would get himself into a self-referential tangle, even an indirect one, and both Socrates and Robert, we can suppose, are innocent of any such folly—being level-headed people, and pious into the bargain—and they make their remark because they take Plato to be uttering a false statement about a quite extraneous topic. If we say, as we surely must, that Robert is right, even though for the wrong reason, does not the principle of equity compel us to say this of Socrates also, since he not only says but thinks the same thing? No, Buridan says, because Socrates, even though unintentionally, has got himself caught in a self-referential situation in which Robert is not involved, so that the utterance of Socrates, unlike that of Robert, must be judged by the severer standards which come into play when we have a case of self-reference. For my own part, I think this last piece of discrimination is just, though Buridan seems to me to misapply it a little. My view would be that the element of self-reference, if it has any effect in this instance, prevents both Socrates and Plato from saying anything whatever—all they do is make a noise—while Robert, making the same noise, does indeed say something by it, but what he says is false. And I'm half inclined to solve this particular puzzle by just throwing the principle of equity to the winds and saying that Plato was wrong and Socrates and Robert right for some quite arbitrary reason, e.g. that Plato was a low Fascist type who has had a bad influence on English philosophy.

This example, however, is only by way of introduction. What I really want to get on to are two *sophismata* which come towards the end of Buridan's chapter, and which involve the notions of knowledge and doubt, and I shall discuss these independently of Buridan.

The first is this. Suppose the following proposition, and nothing else, is written on a wall:

> Socrates knows that the proposition written on the wall is a matter of doubt to him.

By saying that it is a matter of doubt to him, what is meant is of course that he does not know it to be true and does not know it to be false. And suppose that Socrates surveys this proposition for long enough to have grasped its import and if possible made up his mind about it. Is it true or false, and does Socrates know which it is? The answer to this question depends, I think, on how much we assume about Socrates's intelligence. We assume, of course, that whatever he knows is true—this is not an assumption about his intelligence, but just a general truth about knowledge. We may assume also that he can work *modus ponens*, i.e., that if he knows that if p then q, and also knows that p, then he knows that q. We also assume that anything that *we* can find out by inspecting the situation, *he* can find out. Now I suspect that if our assumptions go no further than this, we cannot reach a definite answer to either of our questions. It is worth seeing, all the same, how far they will take us.

In the first place, we can prove that Socrates does not know that the proposition on the wall is true. For if he knows that it is true then it *is* true, and if it is true then he knows that it is a matter of doubt to him, for that is what it says; and if he knows that it is a matter of doubt to him, then it *is* a matter of doubt to him; but if it is a matter of doubt to him then he does not know it. So from the assumption that he knows it we have drawn the conclusion that he does not know it; so he cannot possibly know it. It still, however, might be true, though not known by him to be true; and it might be false, and either known or not known by him to be false. Because of what it says, it is true if and only if it is both a matter of doubt to him and known by him to be so. But he cannot under any circumstances *know that he knows* that it is a matter of doubt to him. For if he knew this, he would know the proposition, and so it would *not* be a matter of doubt to him; and you cannot know that you know what is not the case.

This suggests a further assumption that some might like to make about what Socrates knows. If we add to our previous assumptions the further one that whatever Socrates knows, he knows that he knows, we can give a definite answer to both of our questions. For it will be clear to him, as it is to us, that the proposition is true if and only if he knows that it is a matter of doubt to him. But by our new assumption—which he will make along with us—he will know that it is a matter of doubt to him only if he *knows that he knows* this. But we have just shown this to be impossible—and he can work that out too. The proposition, therefore, is on this assumption, true only if something impossible is true; that is, it is false, and Socrates will know that it is false by employing our own reasoning.

The puzzle which immediately follows this one in Buridan's work is a little more subtle. Suppose that what is written on the wall is the following disjunction:

> Either Socrates is sitting down or the proposition written on the wall is a matter of doubt to Plato.

This time it is supposed that Plato is reading the notice, that Socrates is not visible, and that Plato has no second sight but is otherwise *in omne arte peritissimus et scientia doctissimus*. To obtain an interesting conclusion here we do not in fact need to credit Plato with more than the comparatively small amount of intelligence with which we credited Socrates in our first set of assumptions—we do not need to assume that whatever he knows, he knows that he knows.

Let us consider first whether the proposition on the wall can be false. If it is false then both its disjuncts are false, and in particular the proposition on the wall is *not* in doubt with Plato. That is, if it is false, he either knows that it is false or knows that it is true. But if it is false he cannot know that it is true because it *isn't* true. So if it is false he knows that it is false. And, of course, if he knows that it is false it *is* false. So *it is false if and only if he knows that it is false*—this is an important result; bear it in mind. But can he know that it is false? No, because if he knows that it is false he knows that both of its disjuncts are false and therefore knows that Socrates is not sitting down. But *ex hypothesi* he does not know whether Socrates is sitting down or not. So he does not know that the proposition on the wall is false, and since it is false if and only if he knows it is, it is *not* false, but true. And Plato is just as capable of performing this proof as we are, so he knows that it is true. So he is *not* in doubt about it; that is, the second disjunct is false. And of course he can reach this conclusion too. But he can also do ordinary disjunctive reasoning, and since he knows that the whole disjunction is true and also knows that its second disjunct is false, he knows that its first disjunct is true, that is, he knows that Socrates is sitting down. But *ex hypothesi* he does *not* know this.

We conclude that the conditions we have laid down contain an inconsistency; and as it seems obvious that the other conditions are jointly possible, I think we must say that under these conditions it cannot be written on the wall that either-Socrates-is-sitting-down-or-what-is-written-on-the-wall-is-doubtful-to-Plato. The *words*, of course, may be so inscribed, but from this fact alone nothing of any consequence follows; what our reasoning supposes is that they can under these circumstances be used to assert this thing; and our conclusion is that they cannot. The *same words*, one might add, might be written at the same time on a piece of paper (Buridan introduces this complication, though not into this *sophisma* but the preceding), and these words on the paper *could* mean something, namely that either Socrates is sitting down or what is written on the wall is in doubt with Plato; and, meaning this, their truth or falsehood would depend on whether Socrates is sitting down—the other disjunct being false because nothing is written on the wall, i.e. because for no p is it written on the wall that p.

It is not at all difficult to formalize the language and reasoning employed in this discussion. All we need to do is to supplement the usual Lukasiewicz symbolism for truth-functions with (a) a function Lp, to be read as 'Socrates knows that p' (or 'Plato knows that p,' in the second *sophisma*), (b) a function Wp, to be read as 'It is written on the wall that p,' and (c) a function Ipq, to be read as 'The proposition that p is the same proposition as the proposition that q.' The last is undefined, but has the usual laws for identity, i.e.

A1. Ipp
A2. CIpqCfpfq,

where f is any function of the system which forms a sentence from a sentence. We can then define the function Qp, 'Socrates doubts whether p,' as KNLpNLNp, i.e. Socrates does not know that p and does not know that not p. We can also define the form ipfpgp, to mean 'the proposition p such that fp is such that gp,' e.g. 'the proposition p such that it is written on the wall that p, is such that Socrates knows that p,' i.e. 'Socrates knows that the proposition on the wall is true.' Note that I do *not* write 'g(ipfp),' as this can give rise to scope ambiguities; 'ip' is like a quantifier that is followed by two formulae, as 'For all x if—then—' would be if we used a single prefix for it. I define the form 'ipfpgp,' however, in the usual Russellian way as 'For some p, both (i) for all q, fq if and only if Iqp, and (ii) gp.' If we use 'T' for the proposition 'Socrates is sitting down,' what is written on the wall in the last *sophisma* comes out as

ATipWpQp,

'Either Socrates is sitting down or the proposition p such that it is written on the wall that p, is such that Plato doubts whether p.'

We can abbreviate this to 'S.' The premise that this is what is written on the wall then becomes

A3. ipWpIpS,

i.e. 'The proposition p such that it is written on the wall that p, is such that it, i.e. the proposition that p, is the proposition that S.' The further premise that Plato does not know whether Socrates is sitting down, is, of course,

A4. QT.

Our assumptions about Plato's knowledge come out as

A5. CLpp,
A6. CLCpqCLpLq,

and the rule

RL: If X is a theorem so is LX.

Our reasoning can then be sketched thus:

1. CIpSEfpfS (easily proved from A2)
2. CipWpIpSipWpEfpfS (from 1 by quantification theory)
3. ipWpEfpfS (A3, 2)
4. EipWpfpfS (3, quantification theory)
5. EATipWpQpATQS (4)
6. ESATQS (5, Df.S)
7. ENSNATQS (6)
8. ENSKNTNQS (7)
9. CNSNQS (8)
10. CNSNLS (A5)
11. CNSLNS (9, 10, Df.Q)
12. ENSLNS (11, A5)
13. ELNSLKNTNQS (8, RL, A6)
14. CLNSLNT (13)
15. CLNSNQT (14, Df.Q)
16. NLNS (15, A4)
17. NNS (16, 12)
18. S (17)
19. LS (18, RL)
20. NQS (19, Df.Q)
21. LNQS (20, RL)
22. LATQS (6, 19)
23. LT (21, 22, A6)
24. NQT (23, Df.Q)

The derivability of the contradiction A4, 24 does not mean, of course, that this language is intrinsically inconsistent. Only A1 and A2 belong to logic; the rest of our postulates only state the assumed conditions in the problem, and that they come out in our formalism as inconsistent is a virtue in that formalism, since they *are* inconsistent.

The syntax of this language is in fact extremely straightforward, but its semantics must be admitted to be a bit non-standard, in that certain of its well-formed tokens may be true or false sentences on some occasions—describable in the language—and non-significant on others—also describable in the language. Just because of this peculiarity this language escapes some of the limitations of certain others; and I once suspected that it could be consistently extended to contain its own semantics.

This last rather euphoric conjecture, however, appears to be unfounded. For let us write 'S Means that p' as short for

The one thing that every sentence-token of the type of S means-when-it-means-anything, is that p.

(The proviso 'when it means anything' takes care of those cases where the token falls into meaninglessness through being involved in some paradoxically self-referential situation.) We then define 'What S Means is false' as 'The p such that S Means that p, is such that not p.' It is then quite easy to deduce contradictory consequences from the sentence

A. The sentence on the wall Means that what the sentence on the wall Means is false.

In no circumstances, therefore, is A true; i.e. its negation is, or is an instantiation of, a logical law. But suppose there is written on the wall in question the sentence 'What the sentence on the wall Means is false.' There will then be such an object as *the* sentence on the wall; for 'What the sentence on the wall Means is false' is certainly a sentence of our present language, on the assumption that it contains its own semantics. And this semantics, on the same assumption, will certainly include the rule that 'What the sentence on the wall Means is false' Means that what the sentence on the wall Means is false (i.e. any token of this type which means anything at all, means this). But from these premises, the impossible conclusion A immediately follows. We must conclude, therefore, that 'Means' (and consequently 'means') must be relativised to a lower language than that in which it itself occurs, so that 'what the sentence on the wall Means is false' cannot Mean in L that what the sentence Means in L is false, but can only Mean this in L's metalanguage.

MEANING AND SPEECH ACTS*

JOHN R. SEARLE

A common pattern of philosophical analysis in recent years has been to show that a certain word is associated with certain kinds of speech acts. It is said that the word in question is *used* to perform certain kinds of speech acts or that the word *functions* to perform them. Moreover the statement that a word is used to perform such speech acts is taken by the philosophers who say this sort of thing to be a statement about the meaning of the word, or—which many of them take to be the same thing—to be part of a philosophical analysis or explication of the word.

Here are some examples of this pattern of analysis: R. M. Hare in *The Language of Morals* says, "The primary function of the word 'good' is to commend."[1] He also says the word 'good' has "commendatory meaning" and he says further that it has "evaluative meaning." His remarks about the meaning of 'good' thus associate it with two types of speech acts, commending and evaluating, and these remarks about meaning are based on his remarks to the effect that 'good' is used, or functions, to commend.

P. F. Strawson in his article "Truth" says of the word 'true' that in using it "we are confirming, underwriting, admitting, agreeing with, what somebody has said."[2] In this connection he also mentions certain other speech acts, among them endorsing and conceding. That he takes these remarks about the use of the word to be relevant to the problem of the meaning or explication of the word is at least suggested by his earlier remarks to the effect that the problem of how the word is used is the same problem as "the philosophical problem of truth."[3]

These are two obvious examples of the sort of analysis I have in mind,[4] but the pattern which they exemplify is one which is widely employed. This pattern of analysis involves at least the following. It is claimed in discussing a word W that

---

* Reprinted with revisions and additions, from the *Philosophical Review* of October 1962.
[1] R. M. Hare, *The Language of Morals*, Oxford, 1952, p. 127.
[2] P. F. Strawson, "Truth," in *Philosophy and Analysis*, ed. Margaret Macdonald, Oxford, 1954, p. 272.
[3] *Ibid.*, pp. 260–261.
[4] There are many other examples one might have chosen. I chose these two because they are lucid and because I regard them both as powerful and original contributions to philosophy, in spite of the few misgivings I wish to express.

(1) W is used to perform speech act or acts A.
(2) The statement (1) tells us the meaning or at least part of the meaning of W. (Or alternatively: the statement (1) gives us an explication or analysis or at least part of an explication or analysis of W.)

How shall we construe these theses? Since (2) tells us that (1) is a fact about the meaning of W, it is tempting to construe (1) as saying:

(3) If W occurs in a sentence S and it has its literal meaning in S then characteristically in the utterance of S one performs A.

The difficulty is, though, that this thesis is very easily refuted, for if it is part of the meaning of W that any speaker who utters a sentence containing it, where its occurrence is literal, is characteristically performing act A, then we need only to find contexts where the occurrence of W is literal and the speech act A could not be performed, in order to refute the thesis. And this is not hard to do. For example let us substitute 'good' for W and 'commend' for A. Even if in uttering 'This is a good car' one is commending the car, obviously one is not commending anything in the utterance of the interrogative form 'Is this a good car?'[5] But perhaps this is not a serious counter-example, for someone defending the original analysis could simply argue that just as 'This is a good car' has in part the force of 'I commend this car,' so 'Is this a good car?' (addressed to a hearer) has in part the force of 'Do *you* commend this car?' That is, the alleged counter-example is only a counter-example to (1) and (2) if we take them as implying (3). But instances of (1) such as ' "Good" is used to commend' should not be taken as saying what amounts to an instance of (3), 'For *every* sentence S in which "good" occurs in its literal meaning, an utterance of S is characteristically a *performance* of the act of commendation' (that would be, so to speak, a philistine interpretation). Rather it should be taken as the following:

(4) If a word W (e.g., 'good') occurs in a sentence S and has its literal meaning in S then characteristically when one utters S some speech act A (e.g., commendation) is in the offing. And the way in which it is in the offing will depend on the nature of the sentence. If, for example, S is a simple indicative sentence (e.g., 'This is good') it is performed, if S is interrogative it is (perhaps) elicited; and so on through other forms.

The point of qualifying (3) into (4) is this: the philosophers under discussion are not committed to the view that whenever a word has a literal occurrence a given speech act is *performed*, but only that literal occurrences of the word where the act is not performed can be

---

[5] For a similar argument see Paul Ziff, *Semantic Analysis*, Ithaca, 1960, p. 228.

explained in terms of the cases where it is performed. Of course they do not expect what holds true of indicative sentences to hold true of interrogatives, but the differences will simply be due to the difference between interrogatives and indicatives. What is meant by saying the act is "in the offing" then is simply that the relation of the occurrence of the word to the performance of the act will be in general a function of the nature of the sentence in which the word occurs. Or more explicitly: any departure from the performance of the act will in general be explicable in terms of the way the sentence (and perhaps other features of the context) depart from the standard indicative cases.

Now this I sincerely believe to be a more sympathetic interpretation of what linguistic philosophers must mean when they say that a word W is used to perform speech act A, and consequently I do not think they would regard the interrogative counter-examples as very troubling. Nonetheless I believe that counter-examples can be produced even to (4), counter-examples which may well prove decisive against these theories at least as they were originally intended; and I now propose to do this using 'good' as an example.

It is alleged that in saying, e.g., 'This is a good car' I am uttering something which has at least in part the same use as, or the same function as, or the same force as 'I commend this car.' This, I take it, is a reasonable interpretation of the remark ' "Good" is used to commend'; for a paradigm expression used to commend is 'commend,' or rather 'I commend.' Hence to say 'good' is used to commend is to say 'good' is used something like 'I commend.'

Let me just add parenthetically here that of course 'commend' is being used to do the work of many other verbs, and it will not bear the burden. It would be more plausible and still in the spirit of the analysis to say not just ' "Good" is used to commend,' but ' "Good" is used to commend, praise, express approval, express satisfaction, express appreciation, recommend, etc.,' depending on the context of the utterance. So in the future let us take this expanded version to be the one under discussion and henceforth when we say 'commend' we mean 'commend, etc.'

Now consider the following examples:

(1) If this is a good electric blanket then perhaps we ought to buy it for Aunt Nellie.
(2) I wonder if it is a good electric blanket.
(3) I don't know whether it is a good electric blanket.
(4) Let us hope it is a good electric blanket.

In utterances of each of these one can suppose the occurrence of 'good' to be quite literal, and yet in utterances of none of them are the speech acts of commendation, etc., performed; nor are such speech acts even in the offing in the way they might be supposed to be in the offing for utterances of the interrogative form 'Is this a good electric blanket?'

That is, even if we agreed—and it is not at all clear that we would—that 'Is this a good electric blanket?' had in part the force of or use of or function of 'Do you commend this electric blanket?' still the above do not have the force or use or function of:

(1a) If I commend this electric blanket then perhaps we ought to buy it for Aunt Nellie.
(2a) I wonder if I commend this electric blanket.
(3a) I don't know whether I commend this electric blanket.
(4a) Let us hope I commend this electric blanket.

We began by considering a similarity of function between expressions like 'I commend this electric blanket' and 'This is a good electric blanket.' But this similarity of function is not preserved through the permutations of linguistic context in which each of these expressions can be placed without alteration of the literal meanings of the component words. What is hypothesized in the utterance of the hypothetical 'If I commend this then so and so' is the performance of the action which is *performed* in the utterance of the categorical indicative 'I commend this.' But what is hypothesized in the utterance of 'If this is good then so and so' is not the performance of the action which it is alleged we perform in the utterance of the categorical indicative 'This is good,' for indeed no act or action is here hypothesized at all.

In short, no matter how we try to construe the statement 'The word "good" is used to commend,' as long as we take it as telling us about the meaning of the word 'good' it seems to collapse in the face of such counter-examples as (1)-(4), for these are literal occurrences of the word and the speech acts of commendation, etc., are not in the offing in the relevant ways. And this thesis collapses in a way in which the thesis ' "Commend" is used to commend' does not collapse.

I hope this point is completely clear. If someone tells me something about the *meaning* of a word, then presumably what he tells me should hold true generally of occurrences of the word where it has that literal meaning. If we construe ' "Good" is used to commend' as telling us something about the meaning of 'good' then even under our expanded sympathetic interpretation (4) it does not hold generally for literal occurrences of 'good.' So it seems it must be defective in some respect.

The argument I am using seems to work against any identification of the meaning of a word (which is not a speech-act word like 'commend' or 'confirm' nor an interjection) with some speech act or range of speech acts. Thus even if 'p is true' means something like 'I confirm p' still 'If p is true then q is true' does not mean anything like 'If I confirm p then I confirm q.' So this pattern of philosophical analysis seems to fail.

One of the original grounds for the view I am discussing was an apparent analogy between the use of such philosophically troubling words as 'true,' 'good' and 'know' and certain so called performative verbs, e.g., 'confirm,' 'commend' and 'guarantee.' What I am arguing is that the analogy fails to hold for the sort of examples I have provided. So the sense in which 'true' is used to confirm, 'good' to commend and 'know' to guarantee, seems to be quite different from the sense in which 'confirm' is used to confirm, 'commend' to commend and 'guarantee' to guarantee.

Nonetheless it seems to me there is something true and important in the results produced by the pattern of analysis I have discussed, and now I wish to try to uncover it. (A clue that 'good' is tied to certain speech acts is provided by the fact that in non-philosophical contexts it and certain other words are called terms of praise, suggesting a connection between these words and the speech act of praising.) The first step in my strategy will be to examine how the views in question were arrived at in order that we may see at which point the argument went wrong.

II

Many philosophers believe that the meaning of a word is its use, or is at any rate somehow connected with its use. This is taken to be both the germ of a theory of meaning and a methodological principle of philosophical analysis. As a methodological principle its application consists in transforming any question of the form 'What does W mean?' into 'How is W used?' "Don't ask for the meaning," they say; "ask for the use." But the difficulty with this transformation is that the philosophers who employ it almost invariably confine their discussion of the use of W to the use of sentences of a simple indicative kind which contain W. The transformation occurs as follows. The question

(1) What does W mean?

is taken as equivalent to the question

(2) How is W used?

which is then tacitly interpreted to mean

(3) How is W used in simple categorical indicative sentences of the form, e.g., 'This is W'?

and that is then tacitly taken to be the same question as

(4) How are these sentences containing W used?

and that is taken to mean

(5) What speech acts does the speaker perform in uttering these sentences?

It seems to me the philosophers under discussion offer correct answers to (5) but not necessarily to (1). They take their answers to (5) to be answers to (1) because they suppose that (1) and (2) are the same and they then tacitly interpret (2) so that it generates (3), (4) and (5). But my argument is that their correct answers to (5) cannot be correct answers to (1), and my counter-examples are designed to show that they fail as answers to (1) because the words they are analyzing have literal occurrence where the speech acts which they allege the words are used to perform are not even in the offing in the relevant way. My diagnosis of their mistakes is to show that when they say that W is used to perform speech act A they are not answering the question they take themselves to be answering.

The association of certain words with certain speech acts must seem puzzling in any case since the unit of the speech act is not the word but the sentence. By placing a particular interpretation on the doctrine that the meaning of a word is its use these philosophers have confused the question 'What does such and such a word mean?' with the question 'What speech act is performed in the utterance of such and such a sentence containing that word?'

Another way to put this is as follows. The association between 'good' and commendation does not answer the question 'What does "good" mean?' but instead the question 'What is it to call something "good"?' Thus the old philosophical question 'What is it for something to be good?' or 'What is the nature of the good?' has been confused with the question 'What is it to *call* something good?' The assumption that these two sorts of question are the same is one of the most common mistakes in contemporary philosophy.

We are now in a position to see why my examples are counter-examples to the original thesis. The conclusion, that 'good' is used to commend, was arrived at via a study of what act is performed when something is called good. But in my examples nothing is *called* good. Rather in their utterance it is hypothesized that something is good, the hope is expressed that something is good, and so on.

If we had simply said 'To call something good is to commend it,' my examples would not be counter-examples to the thesis; for hypothesizing, for example, that something gets called good may well be hypothesizing that it gets commended; and so on through the other examples. But, to repeat, the mistake is to suppose that an analysis of calling something good gives us an analysis of 'good.' This is a mistake because any analysis of 'good' must allow for the fact that the word makes the same contribution to different speech acts, not all of which will be instances of calling something good. 'Good' means the same whether I ask if something is good, hypothesize that it is good or just assert that it is good. But only in the last does it (can it) have what has been called its commendatory function.

So far then I have argued that the pattern of philosophical analysis which consists in saying of a word W (where W is not a speech-act word or an interjection) that it is used to perform a speech act A does not give us the sort of information about the meaning of W that certain philosophers have supposed. But I have also argued that it does tell us something true and important, namely that in calling something W one characteristically performs speech act or acts A. Or, to put it another way, in asserting that something is W one is characteristically performing act or acts A.

Now in a paper of this sort one might just stop there—but from what I have said I am left with a residual problem to which I should like to sketch the outlines of a solution.

III

The problem is this: how can it both be the case that it is a non-contingent fact that calling something good is commending it, or something of the sort, and yet that this non-contingent fact does *not* give us the sort of information about the meaning of 'good' that Hare and others seem to have supposed? That is, I take it that it is not just a contingent fact that calling something good is praising it or commending it or the like. It is not, for example, like the fact that calling someone a Communist agent in present day Michigan is insulting or denigrating him. This is a fact about the political attitudes of contemporary Michiganiens and might not hold, say, for employees of the Soviet Embassy in Washington.

But if it is some sort of necessary fact that calling something good is commending it then mustn't this be a necessary fact about the concept *good*, and if that is so, mustn't this fact tell us at least part of the meaning of 'good?' A similar problem could be posed about 'true,' 'know,' etc.

What I have said previously I have offered as a completely general thesis about a whole pattern of analysis in contemporary philosophy. What I am going to say now just concerns the word 'good.' Later I shall briefly discuss 'true' along similar lines.

First I wish to distinguish two classes of speech-act[6] verbs: in group

---

[6] The notion of a speech act employed here and throughout this paper is due to J. L. Austin. The verbs under discussion are called illocutionary verbs in his terminology, and the acts illocutionary acts.

X I include such verbs as 'grade,' 'evaluate,' 'assess,' 'judge,' 'rate,' 'rank' and 'appraise.' In group Y I include such verbs as 'commend,' 'praise,' 'laud,' 'extol,' 'express approval,' 'express satisfaction' and 'recommend.' These two classes are sometimes lumped together, but I think it is clear that they are different. I may evaluate something favourably or unfavourably but I cannot extol it favourably or unfavourably. I may grade it as excellent or bad, but I cannot praise it as bad. Members of group Y thus stand to members of group X in a relation something like the relation of determinate to determinable. To praise something is often or perhaps even characteristically to offer an assessment of it. But not just any kind of assessment, rather a favourable assessment. Not all assessments are favourable.

Now for the purpose of performing acts in the determinable range—assessing, grading, etc.—there is, depending on the subject matter, a range of terms one can use. Thus, e.g., in grading students we use the letters A, B, C, D and F. One of the most common of these grading labels—as Urmson calls them[7]—is 'good.' Other common grading labels are 'excellent,' 'bad,' 'fair,' 'poor' and 'indifferent.' Giving an assessment will characteristically involve among other things assigning a grading label, and conversely assigning one of these will characteristically be giving an assessment, evaluation, or the like. And the term assigned will indicate the kind of assessment made, favourable or unfavourable, highor low, and so on.

The reason that it is a non-contingent fact that calling something good is commending it, or the like, is this: to call it good is to assign it a rank in the scale of assessment or evaluation, but to assign it a rank in this scale is not just to assess or evaluate it; it is to give a particular kind of evaluation of it. In the case of 'good' it is to give it a (fairly) high or favourable evaluation. But giving a high evaluation is characteristically, as I have already suggested, commending or praising, or the like—which of these it is depending on the situation in which the utterance is made.

So the quasi-necessary truth that calling something good is commending it does not tell us the meaning of 'good' but tells us about the way the word is embedded in the institutions of group X and the relations between those institutions and the speech acts in group Y. The connection between the meaning of 'good' and the performance of the speech act of commendation, or the like, though a necessary one, is thus a connection at one remove.

Well, what does 'good' mean anyhow? Anything like a complete answer to this question is beyond the scope of this paper. As Wittgenstein suggested[8] it has like 'game' a family of meanings. Prominent

[7] J. O. Urmson, "On Grading," in *Logic and Language*, Second Series, ed. A. G. N. Flew, Oxford, 1953.
[8] *Philosophical Investigations*, I. 77.

among them is this one: 'meets the criteria or standards of assessment or evaluation.' Other members of the family are: 'satisfies certain interests,' 'satisfies certain needs,' and 'fulfills certain purposes.' (These are not unrelated; that we have the criteria of assessment we do will depend on such things as our interests.) Hare has seen that *saying* that something meets the criteria or standards of evaluation or assessment is giving an evaluation or assessment of a certain kind, namely commendatory.

But the incorrect inference that the meaning of 'good' is therefore somehow explicable in terms of commendation prevents us from seeing what I have been trying to emphasize, that 'good' means the same whether I am expressing a doubt as to whether something is good, or asking if it is good, or saying that it is good. For that reason the question 'What is it to call something good?' is a different question from 'What is the meaning of "good"?'

This conclusion it seems to me is further borne out if we consider words which have uses rather similar to 'good' and which contain the relevant speech-act notions as morphological constituents. I am thinking of such words as 'praiseworthy,' 'laudable,' and 'commendable.' To call something praiseworthy is characteristically to praise it. But saying on this basis that ' "praiseworthy" is used to praise' does not give us the meaning or explicate the word 'praiseworthy.' It only tells us that asserting that something is praiseworthy is performing a certain kind of speech act. But that is a *consequence* of the fact that 'praiseworthy' means what it does, i.e., 'worthy of praise'; it is not an explication of that meaning. The connection between 'praiseworthy' and the speech act of praising is not at all like the connection between the verb 'to praise' and the speech act of praising. 'Good,' I am arguing, is like 'praiseworthy' and not like 'to praise.'

Finally let me add a word about how one would deal with the word 'true' along these lines. The problem is this. How can it be the case both that, as Strawson says, calling something true is somehow characteristically endorsing it, conceding it, confirming it, granting it, or the like, and yet that these remarks do not solve or dissolve what he calls 'the philosophical problem of truth'? The answer, I suggest, might be along the following lines. We characteristically call something true, as Strawson observes, only if a comment, remark, assertion, statement or hypothesis, or the like, has already been made or is at least in some way under consideration; in short, only if a proposition is already in the offing. If your house is on fire I do not rush up to you and announce 'It is true that your house is on fire,' rather I simply say 'Your house is on fire.' The former locution I use only when the proposition that your house is on fire is already under consideration, where the question has already been raised prior to my announcement. But if so then my announcement involving the word 'true' will serve to indicate not only that your house is on fire, but also that the question has been previously raised, and my *affirming* (as opposed to denying) that the proposition is true will serve to indicate that I am in agreement with, or conceding, or endorsing, some other speaker's speech act, the speech act in which he initially raised the question. That is, because we characteristically use the word 'true' only when a proposition is already under consideration, and because a proposition is characteristically put under consideration by the performance of some such speech act as asserting, stating or hypothesizing—because of these two facts, calling something true will place us in a certain relation to that initial speech-act; a relation, e.g., of agreement or endorsement, and conversely in the case of 'not true' a relation of disagreement. All of this tells us what sorts of speech acts we might be performing (among others) when we utter the sentence, e.g., 'It is true that your house is on fire.' But for reasons already stated it still does not tell us the solution to the philosophical problem of truth.

COMMENTS

ZENO VENDLER

The basic dilemma inherent in the view Professor Searle attacks can be stated in quite general terms. On the one hand, it seems to be reasonable to think that the kind of speech act with which a word is characteristically associated is relevant to the meaning of that word. Yet, as Searle points out, the same word can occur in a variety of significant utterances which do not amount to such a speech act and which, moreover, cannot even be explained in terms of its performance.

'Good' and 'excellent' are commonly regarded as words of positive appraisal, words of commendation. Indeed, in most cases, to say that x is good or excellent is to give a favorable verdict on x or to commend x. To ask the question, however, whether x is good, or to deny that x is good, or to assume that x is good is certainly not the same thing as to appraise favorably or to commend x. Moreover, as Searle shows, what is questioned, denied, or assumed in these utterances is not the performance of appraisal or commendation either. One can find other illustrations to the same point which are less notorious philosophically than 'good' or 'true.' For instance the phrase 'nine o'clock' is used to tell the time, or to determine the time of a certain event. Here, again, it would be hard to deny that this piece of information contributes significantly to one's understanding of what that phrase means. Yet to wonder or to ask whether it is nine o'clock is surely not telling the time, or determining the time of some occurrence, nor is such a performance the thing we question or wonder about.

If this is so, then there is a strong temptation to say that since the meaning of a word can be given, at least in part, by specifying the speech act in which it is characteristically used, in utterances that do not amount to or do not depend upon that speech act the word or phrase has a different meaning, or, at least, it falls short of its full meaning. But this conclusion is certainly absurd. The answer 'It is a good blanket' would not be an answer to the question 'Is it a good blanket?' if 'good' meant different things in the two sentences. Again, in that case, to say that it is not a good blanket would not be a formal denial of the assertion that it is a good blanket. Faced with this apparent *reductio ad absurdum*, Searle and others are inclined to reject the claim that the kind of speech act with which a word is associated contributes something to the meaning of the word.

Now I think that this step overcomes the temptation by falling into the contrary sin. Both dangers can be avoided as soon as we realize that, on the one hand, the meaning of a word depends only upon its occurrence in certain types of utterance, yet, on the other hand, the word can occur, with the same literal meaning, in many other types of utterance. In the case of the word 'good,' for example, I maintain that the fact (*if* it is a fact) that the utterance of 'x is good' is normally an act of commendation, justifies the claim that 'good' is a word of commendation, while the fact that the utterance of 'Is x good?' is not a commendation, and does not question a commendation, detracts nothing from the validity of that claim. In other words, the nature and the function of the utterance 'x is good' are relevant to the meaning of the word 'good' in a way that the nature and the function of the utterance 'x is not good,' 'Is x good?' or 'If x is good then ...' are not.

The philosophical position, according to which questions of meaning can be answered in terms of use, may be reduced to two not necessarily unrelated approaches. The first and more general one attempts to account for the meaning of a word by exhibiting all the sentences in which the word can significantly occur and, in addition, by listing all other words that can significantly occur in the same position in the same sentences. In the terminology of Professor P. Ziff, who follows this path, the meaning of a word is a function of its distributive and contrastive sets.[1] Since this view, with some modifications, seems to me to be essentially correct, and since Searle has nothing to say against it directly, I shall adhere to it in arguing my point. The other, and more specific, approach is at issue in Searle's paper. This, as we saw, tries to determine the meaning of at least some words on the basis of the kind of speech act with which the word is characteristically associated. I shall try to defend this second view on the basis of a corrected version of the first and then make some remarks on Searle's criticism.

It would be superfluous and, in a short commentary, impossible to defend the first view. I just point out that it is in agreement with commonsense notions about the meaning of words. Take, for example, a noun. By giving its distributive set we in fact spell out what verbs and what predicates can be ascribed to it, of what verbs it can be the object, and so forth; that is, in the material mode, we specify what can be said about the kind of thing the noun is supposed to denote, what it can do, what can be done with it, and so on. By giving its contrastive set we display the class to which the noun, or respectively, the kind of thing, belongs. That apples can be red but ideas not, that chairs but not apples can be comfortable, that people can sleep but apples cannot, that apples can be eaten but ideas can-

[1] P. Ziff, *Semantic Analysis*, Ithaca, 1960, Ch. V.

not, that both apples and pears can be round and can be eaten, and that both ideas and theories can be conceived of, and so on and so forth, are relevant bits of information contributing to our understanding of what apples, chairs, ideas, and so on are; or, on another level, what the words 'apple,' 'chair,' 'idea,' and so forth, mean. The same thing, *mutatis mutandis*, holds for adjectives, verbs, adverbs, and other significant parts of speech.

The illustrations I just gave turned on word co-occurrences. There are, however, some other, perhaps even more significant features revealed by the distributive and contrastive sets. To begin with, the very fact that a word occurs only in certain positions in the sentences marks the word as a noun, verb, adjective, or whatever. Beyond this, we find a great number of further characteristics as well. 'John sleeps' is a sentence, but 'John holds' is not; again, while we accept 'John holds the book,' we reject 'John puts the book.' Similarly, we have sentences like 'It is good that it is raining,' or 'It is true that it is raining,' but not things like 'It is red that it is raining.' Moreover, although there are both good stories and true stories, only 'This story is good to tell' is a sentence, while 'This story is true to tell' is not. Now it is quite obvious that these structural features are not less important factors in defining the meaning of words than the co-occurrences mentioned above.

By this time it is well known that syntactic structures stand in transformational relations.[2] To mention an example, 'John is a good cook,' 'John cooks well' and 'John is good at cooking' are transforms of one another. We can say, therefore, that part of the difference of meaning between, for instance, 'good' and 'young' is due to the fact that while 'John is a good cook' has those transforms, 'John is a young cook' does not. It follows, then, that the meaning of a word depends on features of co-occurrence, structure and transformation.

Now the next point is crucial to my argument. It is clear that there are linguistic transformations that are restricted to certain kinds of sentence, while others apply to all, or nearly all, sentences of the language. The transformations just mentioned, for instance, are very restricted ones. They apply to sentences like 'John is a good cook,' 'Mary is a good dancer,' 'She is a bad actress,' and so forth, but not to sentences like 'John is a tall man,' 'Mary is a beautiful girl,' 'She is a young actress,' not to speak of totally different sentences like 'The cat is on the mat' or 'I love Lucy.' There are, however, transformations that can operate on all these and practically all other sentences with equal ease. Transformations producing questions, negations and various sentence compounds are the most obvious cases of such unrestricted scope. Every sentence, or nearly every sentence, can be questioned, denied, or connected with other

[2] See, for instance, N. Chomsky, *Syntactic Structures*, The Hague, 1957.

sentences. Accordingly, these transformations do not discriminate among sentences and, consequently, do not discriminate among words either; the knowledge that a word occurs in a sentence that can be questioned, denied or connected with other sentences does not contain any information about the word beyond the triviality that it is a word. To conclude: the possibility of these forms is irrelevant to the meaning of words.

If this is so, then the task of giving the distributive and contrastive sets for a word that accounts for its meaning becomes a simpler task: it will involve only kernel sentences, that is, sentences not yet operated upon by any transformation, and the products of all the restricted, i.e., selective, transformations on these kernels. A little reflection shows that this model is far more in agreement with our ordinary notions of meaning than the one calling for the impossible task of enumerating all the sentences, no matter how complex, that contain the word.

Let us assume, then, that the limited task has been accomplished for a given word. Since the number of kernel types is small, and the vocabulary of the language is finite, the list will start with a finite number of kernel sentences. To these one has to add the products of all the restricted transformations. The result, of course, will be a very large set. It is desirable, therefore, that one should be able to describe the set in terms of some regularities instead of exhibiting it in full. Fortunately, we have a number of terms we can use in describing the set. Saying, for instance, that a word is a noun, we express certain structural and transformational features; adding that it is an animate noun, we draw attention to some regularities of co-occurrence, and so on. With respect to adjectives, too, we classify them as color words, shape words, words of appraisal or commendation (like 'good'), metalinguistic words (like 'true' or 'probable'), and so forth. The selection of these terms may be due to many principles. For instance, in calling 'probable' a metalinguistic adjective, we acknowledge the fact that 'probable,' in the distributive set, can only be ascribed to nominalized sentences (there are no probable tables or horses), and the fact that its contrastive set displays 'true,' 'false,' 'likely,' 'unlikely,' but not 'dolomitic,' 'red,' or 'square.' On the other hand, 'good' or 'excellent' may be called terms of positive appraisal or commendation, if utterances corresponding to the kernels and selective transforms of their distributive set amount to appraisals or commendations. Thus we see that although 'good' may occur in a great number of significant utterances that are not appraisals or commendations, this fact has no influence on the meaning of the word, which remains determined, *for all its occurrences*, by a relevant subset of its possible contexts.

Returning now to Searle's paper, we at once see that all his counter-examples are products of completely general, non-selective transformations. This is quite obvious as to the question 'Is this a good car?' The other four examples, that is,

> If this is a good electric blanket, then . . .
> I wonder if it is a good electric blanket
> I don't know whether it is a good electric blanket
> Let us hope it is a good electric blanket

are again results of completely, or almost completely general transformations. Nearly every sentence can fit into the frames 'If p then . . . ,' 'I wonder if p,' 'I don't know whether p,' 'Let us hope that p.' For this reason the fact that 'good' appears in these frames is utterly irrelevant to the question what 'good' means. What remains relevant, however, is its occurrence in sentences like

> This is a good blanket
> He is a good dancer
> He is good at dancing
> This soup is good to eat
> It is good of him to come
> It is good that it is raining

and so on, since these forms involve selective structures and selective transformations (for by substituting, say, 'red' for 'good,' we spoil most of these sentences). Now if it turned out that all the sentences determining the meaning of 'good' were such that their utterance amounted to a commendation, then the statement of this regularity would be an extremely valuable factor in an attempt to "give" the meaning of the word without spelling out its distributive and contrastive sets in full detail. Unfortunately, there are good reasons to think that some of these sentences are not commendatory. What do I commend when I say that it is good that it is raining? Nevertheless, it is true that most of these sentences have a commendatory use. And even this tells me something about the meaning of 'good.'

COMMENTS*

PAUL BENACERRAF

First of all, I would like to say that I am with Mr. Searle in spirit. I agree with most of what he says. But it is unseemly and certainly dull for a commentator to express nothing but agreement. I will therefore limit such expressions to the foregoing.

In his paper, Mr. Searle discusses what certain philosophers have said concerning the use or uses of certain words and phrases. He is concerned with the view that to state that a given speech act is performed in using some word (or words) is to state or make a statement about the meaning of that word (or those words). Taking interjections and certain speech-act words as exceptions, he attempts to refute this view. The particular quarries he hunts are Hare, in *The Language of Morals* (" 'Good' is used to commend"), and Strawson, in an apparent misnomer, "Truth" (" 'True' is used to express agreement").

Limiting my attention to section I of Searle's paper, I will argue as follows: (A) That the view he attacks may not be as widely held as we are led to suppose, (B) that he fails to refute it, and (C) that his general negative thesis concerning the relation of speech acts and meaning is false, for sometimes, to state that a given speech act is performed in using some word or words, *is* to state the meaning of that word or those words, even when they are neither interjections nor speech-act words. In a final section, (D), I will try to state briefly how I think some of these matters should be viewed.

(A) My first objection, then, is quasi-historical and concerns matters of interpretation. I think that the view presented as the Strawsonian view is best described, following Quine, as the Strawmanian view. First of all, in "Truth" Strawson, with but a few lapses, is generally careful to attribute the function of expressing agreement not to the word 'true' but to whole utterances such as 'That's true' or 'What the policeman said was true.' Secondly, although he quite evidently holds the view concerning 'That's true' which Searle attributes to him, he neither says nor holds that this is a view *about the meaning* of 'true' or 'That's true.' He is talking about what he calls 'the use' of expressions (whatever that may be) and eschewing all talk of meaning—so he cannot in all fairness be

---

* I am grateful to my colleagues George Pitcher and Robert Nozick for reading an earlier draft of these comments and for making many valuable suggestions. The responsibility for any remaining errors is, of course, my own.

accused of the alleged sin. In fact, I doubt if many really can, simply because most people who are inclined to say the likes of 'W is used to X' (with the blanks suitably filled in) are strongly disinclined to speak of 'the meaning of W.' The discussion of the use of words is normally not an entering wedge of the discussion of meaning but rather a substitute for it. The usual accompanying move is this: "Talk of meaning is confused and unhelpful metaphysical claptrap: let's look at the facts; let's look at the use." In short, I suspect that the "common pattern of philosophical analysis of recent years" to which Searle alludes is not so common as all that.

But in defending Strawson and Hare from the charges brought against them, I am not subscribing to their positions. I think merely that if we are to hang them, we should do so for a crime they commit. The crime they commit is not, as Searle supposes, that of thinking that in giving some aspects of the use of an expression they give the meaning; it is rather that of too hastily dismissing the notion of meaning and thereby trying to do without an analytical tool which could be of great use. To say that 'good' is used to commend, is to give some information about the word. Just *what* is being said is not clear, and it is perfectly obvious, as Searle, Ziff, and others point out, that such a statement about 'good' leaves much of the distribution of the word in the language unexplained. If Searle's objections to this "pattern of philosophical analysis" come down to pointing out that more needs to be said before all the important questions which we might raise about 'good' are answered, then I agree wholeheartedly. Much more needs to be said.

(B) My second objection is of a more systematic nature. It is that, false and untenanted as these positions are, Searle's arguments fail to *establish* their falsity. He tries to show that ' "Good" is used to commend' does not tell us about the meaning of 'good' *because* under the only interpretation of ' "———" is used to commend' under which this formula can be taken to be about the meaning of '———,' ' "Good" is used to commend' turns out false but ' "I commend" is used to commend' turns out true. His argument goes as follows (much of this will be paraphrase):

1. Construe ' "Good" is used to commend' as (substituting Searle's formula now)

   (4) If 'good' occurs in a sentence S and has its literal meaning in S then characteristically when one utters S the speech act of commendation is in the offing. If S is a simple indicative, it is performed, if S is interrogative, it is elicited, etc.

2. But 'I commend' is the paradigm expression used to commend; therefore,

3. To say 'good' is used to commend is to say that 'good' is used something like 'I commend.'

4. But consider, e.g.,

   (3) I don't know whether it is a good electric blanket

   and

   (3a) I don't know whether I commend this electric blanket.

   In (3) the speech act of commending is neither performed *nor in the offing*, while, although it is not performed in (3a), it *is* in the offing *there*. Therefore,

5. ' "I commend" is used to commend' when thus construed is true, but ' "Good" is used to commend,' so construed, is false. I quote:

   In short, no matter how we try to construe the statement 'The word "good" is used to commend,' as long as we take it as telling us about the meaning of the word 'good' it seems to collapse in the face of such counter-examples as (1)-(4), for these are literal occurrences of the word and the speech acts of commendation, etc. are not in the offing in the relevant ways. And this thesis collapses in a way in which the thesis ' "Commend" is used to commend' does not collapse.

We are presented with a dilemma: either these statements ' "Good" is used to commend' and ' "True" is used to confirm' are false or they cannot be interpreted as telling us about the meanings of the words in question. It is evident that the argument hangs entirely on whether or not in the cases of (3) and (3a) and the like, acts of commendation are *in the offing*; and I literally do not know what it is for there to be acts *in the offing*.[1] Suppose Searle's hypo-

---

[1] This is not quite so; I think that to say that an act is "in the offing" is to say something very much like that it is about to be performed. But under this interpretation the thesis collapses of its own weight. This is evidently not what Searle means, but the further elucidation we are provided is not much better. For example, how are we to decide if an act of commendation is in the offing in the following (simple indicative) case of a man decrying his own poor judgment?
 (a) I commend what is worthless.
Surely, in this simple indicative case he is not commending. But how are we to explain this "departure from the performance of the act . . . in terms of the way the sentence (and perhaps other features of the context) depart from standard indicative cases"? What is a standard indicative case? What measure of control is to be imposed to distinguish when "explanations of departures" will be *ad hoc*? This is so vague as to be virtually unintelligible. I agree with Searle that *some* principle making the meaning of the whole utterance a function of the meaning of its parts is necessary. But in stating (4) he has not provided one. Every clause is so "hedged" that it is impossible to use this principle to show that anything fails to satisfy it. But his whole argument rests on this. The trouble is, of course, that Searle is trying to give a "knock-down" argument for his case in the space of a couple of pages, and the issues involved are much too complex to permit of such hasty treatment.

thetical opponent, Rabson, argued as follows:

> Searle, you are confusing the issue. Let me give you a trilemma to your dilemma. I will argue that under your suggested interpretation either (a) 'Good' *is* used to commend, i.e., an act of commendation is in the offing, or (b) 'I commend' is *not*, in either case your argument breaks down by failing to show a relevant difference, or (c) your criterion (4) is useless for sorting out the statements that tell us about the meanings of words from those which do not (in which case failing to satisfy it is hardly proof of anything relevant to the issues at hand).
>
> Consider the following statement:
>
> (3b) I don't know whether it is a commendable electric blanket.
>
> Now surely 'commendable' is used to commend. In fact, 'commendable' is very similar in meaning to 'good'; they are of course not exact synonyms, but nevertheless quite close. Now, either there is an act of commendation in the offing in connection with (3b), or there is not. If there is, then I see no reason for denying that there was also one in the offing in connection with (3), where 'good' replaced 'commendable' and this is because of the similarity in meaning between the two words. I submit that the initial plausibility of such a denial really rested on the difference in *syntactic structure* between the simple adjective 'good' and the subject-predicate expression 'I commend,' with which it was being compared. Remove this difference by switching from 'I commend' to 'commendable' and this initial plausibility disappears.
>
> If, however, one insists that there is *no* act of commendation in the offing in connection with (3b), then I see no adequate reason for supposing that such an act *is* in the offing in connection with (3a). Certainly a comparison of (3a) with (3b) will yield no sure way of distinguishing between them *on the point of whether or not there is an act of commendation in the offing*. But if we decide that in none of the three cases is there an act of commendation in the offing, then your argument hardly establishes what it sets out to establish. For no relevant difference has been shown to exist between ' "Good" is used to commend' and ' "I commend" is used to commend.' Certainly no argument has been offered for the view that failing to pass this test is *per se* proof of anything. The only glimmer of an argument *for* the interpretation (4) is that it provides a test which ' "Good" is used to commend,' fails but which ' "I commend" is used to commend' passes. Nothing whatever has been said to support the view that (4) represents a necessary condition for a statement of the form 'W is used to X' to be about the meaning of W.

By this argument I think that Rabson has succeeded in sufficiently muddying the waters to establish my point. The concept of "there being a speech act in the offing" is hardly able to bear the burden placed upon it. But with it sinks the usability of the crucial criterion (4), since it is on *that* clause of the criterion that its use always depends.

(C) What about the general principle Searle attempts to establish? There are many things that *cannot* be done in stating what speech act or acts some word or words may be used to perform. Is stating the meaning of those words one of them? I think not, for consider the following example:

(i) 'Good' is used to perform the speech act of uttering a word meaning 'answering to certain interests.'

Now (i) is a statement attributing the performance of a certain speech act to the use of the word 'good.'[2] And it purports to tell us precisely the meaning of that word. If it fails; this is certainly not because it attributes the performance of some speech act to the use of 'good.' It is because it misstates the meaning of 'good.'

If it be objected that it was not statements *explicitly* about the meanings of words, that Searle has in mind, then I suggest that most likely what he means is that statements associating the performance of certain speech acts with certain words or groups of words *but not explicitly about the meanings of those words*, are not explicitly about the meanings of those words. For even such statements can tell us something about the meaning of the word, or give us information about it. Who can deny that ' "Good" is used to commend' tells us *something* about the meaning of 'good'? It doesn't *state* what that meaning is—but neither is it totally uninformative.

For much the same reasons, there was no reason to conclude, as Searle seems to have done, that ' "I commend" is used to commend' *does* tell us the meaning of 'I commend.' It seems to be a linguistic accident that words characteristically used to talk about or refer to the act of commendation should also be usable to perform it, or that the paradigm of commendation should be 'I commend X,' if indeed it is. That Searle accepts this as demonstrating a difference between 'good' and 'I commend' on the point of whether ' "——" is used to commend' tells us the meaning of '——,' is surprising in the light of the lesson he wants to teach us, e.g., that 'Hello' and not 'I greet' is the paradigm greeting, and 'I insult ——' normally cannot be used

---

[2] Some might object that although (i) does indeed attribute the performance of a speech act to the use of a word and tell the meaning of that word at the same time, the act in question is not an *illocutionary* act, and that although Searle never restricts his thesis to illocutionary acts (he does mention them in another context), this is what he must mean. But it is easy to generate similar counter-examples in terms of illocutionary acts. Consider, for example, possible substitutions in

(ii) '— W —' is used to explain the meaning of 'W.'

to insult. Some speech-act words are "explicit performatives," others are not. If Searle's criterion were clear enough to be usable, there is little reason to believe that it would select out anything but the "explicit performatives." There is no reason to believe that it would achieve its avowed purpose of selecting for us words which when put into the first slot of 'W is used to X' turn it into a statement of their meaning. Statements of the form 'W is used to X' normally do not tell us the meaning of W; when true they tell us one of the things W is used to do.

In fact, if asked to point out the principal insight contained in part I of Searle's paper, I would say that it was this: from the fact that some word (or words) can truly be said to be usable to perform a certain speech act, *normally* nothing or next to nothing follows about the meaning of the word(s) in question. Unlike Searle, I think this applies not only to 'good' but also to 'I commend.' What he would have us take as exceptions—cases in which W is (for example) the first person singular present indicative of the verb that occurs in the place of 'X'—I do not think should be so taken. They too just tell us one of the things that the locution in question is used to do (and I do not pretend to be clear myself about the matter of the *use* of an expression). In fact, they tell us possibly even less, because if you do not know what W means, when W is the verb in the form 'I X,' you are not likely to be much instructed about its meaning by being told that it is used to X. If on the other hand you know the meaning of W, then it might very well be instructive about its *use* to be told that it is used to X, for not every speech-act verb can be used to perform the speech act it denotes.

(D) *Conclusion*. What is the upshot of the above remarks? Well, as I have already suggested, I think that a systematic analysis of meaning, of speech acts, and of how they are related is needed if we are to make the sound points that Searle wishes to make while avoiding what I have argued are the pitfalls which he encounters along the way. I shall now try briefly to indicate the kind of account that I would favor.

1. Utterances—not words nor, as Searle suggests, sentences—are the units of speech acts. Utterance parts can be said to be used to perform such acts, but only derivatively and possibly only elliptically. The correct attribution to an utterance part, of a part of the function served by the whole utterance, is a difficult problem indeed. Many of the most important questions in a general theory of language are involved in its solution.

2. Just about anything that can be done in or by producing an utterance is a speech act. And to whatever degree it is unclear whether so-and-so was done "in or by producing" a given utterance, to just that degree it is unclear whether or not such-and-such a

speech act was performed. It follows that some statements attributing the performance of certain speech acts to given token utterances may be as far from, or come as close as one likes to being, true statements about the meanings of the parts of the utterance: some will be about the tokens, others not. Those that are may be stating their meaning, or may not. Those that do not may nevertheless provide valuable information about their meaning, or they may not. For example, it is to attribute the performance of a certain speech act to the utterance of W to say that to utter W is to utter a sequence of words whose last member is the seventeenth word of Searle's paper. That does not tell us much about the meaning of any of the words uttered. But to utter a sequence of words in that respect like W is to perform a particular speech act. It also follows that on this view the concept of a speech act *per se* is not a terribly important one for linguistic theory. It certainly would not occupy a central part in my scheme. At best it can be seen as indicating an area for further study.

3. On the relation between meaning and speech acts in general, it seems evident that in many cases *that* an utterance may be used to perform certain speech acts is *explainable* on the basis of its meaning. There are some speech acts which are more or less evidently performed, and on the basis of these (*inter alia*) we construct our hypotheses concerning the meaning of expressions. These acts are part of the observational basis for the theoretical account of the language—the statement of the meaning being best regarded as a theory devised to explain such data.

It is in this way that I feel that these matters are best viewed, and I am quite certain that this is not incompatible with what Mr. Searle would want to say.

REJOINDERS

JOHN R. SEARLE

I am in sympathy with some of what Vendler and Benacerraf have to say, but I think much of their apparent disagreement with me rests on misunderstandings.

Vendler presents a detailed argument to show that the mere fact that 'good' occurs in sentences generated by completely general, non-selective transformations of the kind I consider, is irrelevant to the question what 'good' means. I am not in disagreement with this conclusion, nor is it inconsistent with what I say. However Vendler also draws from this argument the quite different conclusion that a study of the *semantic conditions* associated with such examples is irrelevant to the question what 'good' means. This conclusion does not follow from Vendler's argument, nor from his first conclusion, and I am in disagreement with it.

I think that such examples provide a good testing ground for hypotheses concerning meaning, and I think this for a reason both Vendler and I accept, namely that any meaning analysis must show how a word makes the same contribution to different kinds of utterances.

Let us suppose that in studying a word W we find that utterances of certain kernel sentences and certain selective transforms are performances of speech act A. Suppose further that we take this fact as a hypothesis explicatory of the meaning of W. We can test this hypothesis by examining the non-selective transforms to see whether the way these sentences are related to A is purely a function of the nature of the transformations. If not, then the hypothesis is defective and the performance of A in the utterance of the kernel sentence is not to be explained solely on the basis of the meaning of W but must involve other factors as well.

To put this point more generally: If the statement that W is used to perform act A is to be explicatory of the meaning of W, then the relation of any transformation sentence of the distributive set for W to act A must be purely a function of the way the transformation sentence differs from its kernel. This would have to be the case in order that we be able to explain how the word makes the same contribution to the kernel sentences (in whose utterance the act is performed) and to their non-selective transforms (in whose utterance the act is not in general performed).

What a study of my examples shows is that although the performative verbs satisfy (or come close to satisfying) this condition the other words, 'good,' 'true,' etc., do not. What is hypothesized in the utterance of the hypothetical transformation 'If I commend this then . . .' is the act which is performed in the utterance of the kernel 'I commend this.' But what is hypothesized in the utterance of the transform 'if this is good then . . .' is not the act which is performed in the utterance of the kernel 'this is good.'

I am here only repeating in Vendler's terminology points I made in the paper. I think he may be inclined to overlook these in part because he seems to be attributing to me a view which I do not hold, and which I characterize as involving "a philistine interpretation." He seems to think I am troubled by the fact that there are sentences whose utterances would not constitute the performance of the act in question. But that is not my point at all. My point is that there are occurrences which are not even related to the act in the way they would have to be in order that the proposed explication of the word be an explication of its meaning.

Of course I am not saying that such remarks as ' "Good" is used to commend,' ' "True" is used to confirm,' etc. tell us *nothing at all* about the meaning of 'good' and 'true.' On the contrary, in section III I try to suggest what they do tell us.

Benacerraf makes three objections to my paper, designated (A), (B), and (C). I think (A) is mistaken and (B) and (C) rest largely on misunderstandings which I should like to clear up.

(A) He says the philosophers I am criticising are disinclined to speak of the meanings of words because they regard the notion of meaning as "metaphysical claptrap." Strawson in particular he says is "eschewing *all* talk of meaning" (my italics). But consider Strawson's statement (p. 275): "The point of using Austin's word ['performatory'] at all is the fact that the phrase 'is true' can sometimes be replaced, without any important change in *meaning*, by some such phrase as 'I confirm it,' which is performatory in the strict sense" (my italics). This single quotation seems to refute Benacerraf's view concerning Strawson. (Incidentally it also seems to refute his additional view that Strawson is not attributing the performatory function to 'is true' but to whole sentences.) Furthermore a quick glance through Strawson's article will reveal numerous occurrences of the notion of meaning. I am unable to find any textual evidence in Strawson or any of the other relevant authors to suggest that they regard talk of meaning as "metaphysical claptrap." What I do find is the quite different view that the correct way to analyse the meaning of a term is to examine its use, and it is to one application of that principle that my paper is devoted.

(B) The first two horns of Rabson's trilemma are based on a misinterpretation of my unsatisfactory phrase 'in the offing.' However nothing in my article hinges on this phrase as such, since I offer an explanation of how I intend it and then further illustrate it with examples. If the phrase still misleads, as it apparently does, let us drop it altogether and substitute the explanation. Rabson is saying only that he can construe the phrase 'in the offing' so that 'good' satisfies the conditions set by (4). I don't deny that; I only assert that according to the way I have explained (4), 'good,' 'true,' etc., fail to satisfy the conditions, whereas 'commend' and the other performative verbs do satisfy them, and therefore the apparent analogy fails between 'good,' etc., and the relevant performative verbs. This eliminates the first two horns of the trilemma, but at this point Rabson raises the third: Why should we accept (4), so construed, as relevant to the analysis of meaning? But I answered this in the text: "The philosophers under discussion are not committed to the view that whenever a word has a literal occurrence a given speech act is performed, but only that literal occurrences of the word where the act is not performed can be explained in terms of cases where it is performed...." If such passages were not clear perhaps the following will help to clarify them: Some of the philosophers who explicated expressions by saying they were used to perform certain speech acts pointed out that the occurrences of the word where the speech act was performed were the "primary" occurrences of the word. What I take it they meant by that was that the cases where the act was not performed could be explained in terms of the cases where it was, and that the converse did not hold. However, if we try to explicate a word by saying that it is used to perform a certain speech act, and if the word has literal occurrences where the act is not performed and which *cannot* be explained in terms of the cases where it is, then our explication is a failure because it fails to account for those cases (see my discussion of Vendler's paper above). Thus (4) as I have explained it sets a minimum condition for any such explication.

Rabson's argument must seem extraordinarily paradoxical anyhow since he presents an argument which I use to support my thesis as if it were a counter-example. I point out in section III that 'good' means something like 'commendable' or 'praiseworthy' or 'laudable,' and thus I contrast its meaning with that of 'I commend.' Rabson presents the similarity of 'good' and 'commendable' as if it showed the similarity of 'good' and 'I commend.' But this is just to repeat the confusion I have been pointing out. The fact that 'good' is used to commend and 'I commend' is also used to commend does not show the relevant similarity between 'good' and 'I commend.' For the way 'good' is used to commend is like the way 'commendable' is used to commend, not like the way 'I commend' is used to commend. To repeat: the aim of the analysis I am criticizing was to draw an analogy between certain performative verbs and certain philosophically troubling words such as 'good' and 'true' (consider, e.g., the passage quoted from Strawson above). I try to show, in part I, where and why the analogy breaks down, and I try in part III to show the source of the appearance of analogy.

Nor is all this simply a consequence of syntactical considerations. It is crucially important that the addition of the suffixes 'able' and 'worthy' are needed to convert the verbs 'commend' and 'praise' into near synonyms of 'good.' Furthermore not all syntactically appropriate expressions will go through the permutations we are considering. Consider Toulmin's example 'probably.' We say 'Probably p' but not 'If probably p then q'; rather we shift to 'If it is probable that p then q.' It is therefore not clear that my pattern of counter-examples will work for Toulmin's analysis of 'probably,' even though the fact that it is an adverb suggests that it should.

I think Rabson's trilemma fails and I think Benacerraf shows an awareness of this in the appended footnote. But there he turns to a new attack, presenting the apparent counter-example 'I commend what is worthless.' But such examples raise no serious difficulty. The expression 'what is worthless' provides us with a clue, as Benacerraf intends it to, that the sentence would not normally be used to commend. What Benacerraf apparently wants me to provide is some purely structural criterion for isolating all indicative cases where the act is performed from those where it is not. I doubt that such a simple criterion is possible, though Austin's criterion—can one insert 'hereby' between subject and verb, as in e.g. 'I hereby commend' or the like?—is a good rough-and-ready criterion and will suffice to deal with this example.

Section (C) rests on attributing to me no less than four positions I do not state or hold:

(1) I do not hold the general negative view he ascribes to me except insofar as it applies to the pattern of analysis which I discuss.

(2) I am confining my discussion of speech acts to illocutionary acts and I explicitly say so in a footnote.

(3) I do not hold the view that ' "Good" is used to commend' tells us nothing whatever about the meaning of 'good.' Indeed I devote section III of my paper to explaining in what respect it does. My point is that it does not tell us what the philosophers in question thought it did.

(4) I do not hold the view that all illocutionary verbs are the paradigm expressions used to perform the associated speech acts. I only state that 'I commend' is a paradigm expression used to commend. It is doubtful that 'insult' is a counter-

example to the view I do not hold, as it seems to be in part perlocutionary. Better counter-examples are 'hint' and 'insinuate' as they seem to be genuine illocutionary verbs, though it is by no means certain that they are.

I am in sympathy with most of the programmatic portions of Benacerraf's concluding section.

WITTGENSTEIN ON CRITERIA*

NEWTON GARVER

Grammar and Criteria

The concept *criterion* is almost as important in Wittgenstein's later philosophy as *grammar*, and equally bewildering. It is introduced in the *Blue Book* (pp. 24–25) with a flourish of qualification that invites exegesis, and it occurs prominently in many arguments.[1] In attempting to explain what Wittgenstein means by 'criterion' I shall be assuming that the concepts of *criterion* and *grammar* are intimately connected, and that together these concepts are at the core of Wittgenstein's later logical theory.[2] That *criterion* is a concept whose primary use is in the criticism of thoughts or arguments—i.e., is logical—is apparent at every occurrence of the term 'criterion.' That it is intimately connected with *grammar* is equally certain, and can be supported both by textual citations and by considering the logical theory implicit in the *Philosophical Investigations*.

In the *Blue Book*, just prior to his rough explanation of the term 'criterion,' Wittgenstein says: "... to explain my criterion for another person's having toothache is to give a grammatical explanation about

---

* *Editor's note*: In this symposium and the following one, many references are made to Ludwig Wittgenstein's *Philosophical Investigations*, Oxford, 1953 or 1958. For simplicity most of these references are placed within the texts of the symposium papers. But whether within the texts, or in the footnotes, references to numbered sections of Part I of this work are given in the form, e.g., '*Inv*. I. 217,' or where the work need not itself be named, simply 'I. 217'; and references to pages in Part II are given analogously. Wherever context permits further simplification, the specifying of Part I or Part II is omitted as well.

In Mr. Garver's references three other abbreviations occur: '*BBB*' referring to Wittgenstein's *Blue and Brown Books* (Joint ed.), Oxford, 1958; '*D*' referring to Norman Malcolm's monograph *Dreaming*, London, 1959; and '*KOM*' referring to Malcolm's paper, "Knowledge of Other Minds" in *Journal of Philosophy*, LV, 1958, pp. 969–978.

[1] It may be useful to record that the word 'criterion' or 'criteria' occurs one or more times on each of the following pages in *The Blue and Brown Books*: 2, 24, 25, 49, 51, 55, 57, 61, 63, 64, 88, 94, 104, 120, 121, 122, 132, 135, 138, 140, 144. In the *Investigations* 'criterion' or 'criteria' occurs in the following paragraphs of Part I: 51, 56, 141, 146, 149, 159, 160, 164, 182, 185, 190, 238, 239, 253, 258, 269, 288, 290, 322, 344, 354, 377, 385, 404, 509, 542, 572, 573, 580, 625, 633, 692, and in Part II on pages 181, 185, 198, 203, 211, 212, 222. There are also numerous other passages (e.g., *Inv*. I. 145, 154–156, 270, 313) in which criteria are discussed without the word being used.

[2] After all Wittgenstein does have views, if not formally systematic ones, about the nature of philosophical problems, about what language is, and about what gives meaning or significance to linguistic utterances. What I refer to when I speak of "Wittgenstein's logical theory" is his view about the ultimate arbiter of the propriety or significance of utterances and inferences—i.e., about the bedrock at which "my spade is turned." (*Inv*. I. 217)

the word 'toothache,' and, in this sense, an explanation concerning the meaning of the word 'toothache' " (p. 24). Here we find 'criterion,' 'grammar,' and 'meaning' all together, and their juxtaposition presents at a glance what is characteristic in Wittgenstein's later approach to logical theory. A close association between these concepts is reiterated in his remark about the discontent of "the metaphysician" with our "grammar" and with "the common criteria—the criteria, i.e., which give our words their common meanings" (pp. 56-57) and again when he discusses the ordinary prerequisites for understanding the sentence 'I am pointing to my eye' (pp. 63-64).

Wittgenstein's continuing intention that these concepts should be understood together is apparent at several places in the *Investigations*. When, for example, he discusses "the grammar of 'to fit,' 'to be able,' and 'to understand'," he says: "The criteria which we accept for 'fitting,' 'being able to,' 'understanding,' are much more complicated than might appear at first sight. That is, the game with these words, their employment in the linguistic intercourse that is carried on by their means, is more involved—the role of these words in our language other—than we are tempted to think" (I. 182). Here the criteria for certain terms are presented as determining, or prominently influencing—very nearly as being identical with—the "grammar" of those terms. (See also II. 185.) In the remarks on various sorts of states, we find: "But in order to understand the grammar of these states it is necessary to ask: 'What counts as a criterion for anyone's being in such a state?' " (I. 572). The powerful remark, "*Essence* is expressed by grammar" (I. 371), may also be cited; for although it does not explicitly mention criteria, the *least* we must know if we understand the essence of something is the criterion or criteria for it. There is, then, strong textual support for regarding *grammar* and *criterion* as companion concepts in Wittgenstein's later philosophy.

Further exegetical consideration reinforces this view. The concept *grammar*, supported by related concepts, is important in Wittgenstein's attack upon the claim of formal logic to be the sole arbiter of propriety in discourse and argument. The case against the view that logic, in this broad sense, must operate according to strict rules, with no vagueness or imprecision, is presented in a series of remarks in the *Investigations* (I. 65-103). In the place of the mathematical precision of formal logic Wittgenstein emphasizes "grammar," which rests upon an agreement in the way people act, upon a form of life. These remarks about logical theory are constantly presupposed and accented in the following discussions. Thus about certain propositions of which "I can't imagine the opposite" Wittgenstein does not, in the *Investigations*, say that they are "analytic" or "tautologous"—these terms being strongly identified with formal logic through Frege's *Grundlagen* and his own earlier *Tractatus*—but that they are "grammatical" (I. 251). The principal reason for examining 'criterion' in the light of Wittgenstein's conception of grammar is that sometimes we can also refer to criteria in order to decide about the propriety of an utterance or of an argument: virtually every occurrence of the term 'criterion' in the later work is in connection with a question about the propriety of some utterance or about the circumstances in which some utterance is appropriate, and in some of these passages (e.g., I. 160, 625, 633, 692) the utterance in question would seem to express an inference. Thus the concept *criterion* is a logical tool, and as such must be part and parcel of the revised conception of logic in Wittgenstein's later philosophy.

Wittgenstein's use of the term 'grammar' is itself in need of a detailed exposition, so as to make clear its connections both with "the mastery of a technique" (I. 199) and with those matters of grammar (e.g., morphology and syntax) which are the concern of linguistics. Nonetheless the perspective I have chosen appeals to me as the one most likely to throw a non-distorting light on Wittgenstein's position.

The Distinctive Features of Criteria

The distinctive features of Wittgensteinian criteria can be set out in a series of "grammatical propositions" (cf. I. 251). Any of the italicized statements which follow might, in appropriate circumstances, be used as a grammatical explanation of 'criterion,' i.e., to explain what criteria are.

1. *Criteria are human instruments.* A good way to begin is by identifying the genus, so to speak, to which criteria belong. If we are asked what *kind* of thing a criterion is, to say that it is an instrument of a certain sort would be as good an answer as any. The dictionary tells us that a criterion is a test or standard or canon of correctness, and I do not believe that Wittgenstein departed from this basic sense of the word. A standard is an instrument, although not the most common sort. The particular standard kilogram in Paris, for example, is an instrument of a certain sort, although not exactly the sort one uses ordinarily for measurements. Not all tests or standards are used in the same way as the standard kilogram, but it is not difficult to see them all as "instruments of a certain sort"—human contrivances with characteristic uses.

An instrument can be characterized in two different ways: we can speak either of its typical uses or of its typical shape, dimensions, and component materials. In the case of many tools both a functional characterization and a physical description seem important for understanding what such an instrument is. A scythe, for instance, is for mowing grasses and grains, and it has a certain curvature and size that distinguish it from other mowing tools; both aspects of what a scythe is are mentioned by the entry in the Merriam-Webster dictionary. In other cases, however, it is neither essential nor even useful to give a physical description in addition to a functional characterization in the course of explaining what a certain sort of tool or instrument is. A pump, for example, is "a device or machine that raises, transfers, or compresses fluids or that attenuates gases, esp. by suction or pressure, or both." In this case it appears that only the functional aspects are essential to something's being a pump, and that what physical characteristics a pump may have is, as it were, an incidental matter. It is not always easy to say what is essential (cf. I. 62), and physical characteristics may assume a pre-eminent importance if the question is one of distinguishing two kinds of pumps, rather than of explaining what a pump is. Nevertheless, *some* functional characterization is always essential to an explanation of what some instrument is; where none can be given, as in the case of certain objects from anthropologists' diggings, it remains an open question whether the artifact is an instrument or an ornament.

It is important to realize that this initial characterization of criteria is only a very short step forward. Its import is mostly negative; it warns us against identifying criteria in every respect with the circumstances of phenomena out of which these instruments may be fashioned, and against divorcing them from their characteristic roles in human intercourse. We must also bear in mind that the variety of items which might fall under the label 'Tools and Instruments' is very great, and criteria should not be too closely associated in our thoughts with any of the others. We still have to say much more in order to make clear what sort of instrument a criterion is.

2. *Criteria govern the use of certain linguistic expressions.* This second step is an attempt to answer the question "What are these instruments for?" At this point we begin to distinguish Wittgensteinian criteria from the rest.

At first it may seem that our answer to this question is at odds with the way Wittgenstein actually talks; for questions are raised in the *Investigations* about criteria for all sorts of different things—for a person's being of a certain opinion (I. 573), for someone's being in a state of expectation (I. 572), for a person's reading (I. 164), for 'fitting,' 'being able to,' and 'understand' (I. 182), for something's being a matter of course for me (I. 238), for the identity of sensations (I. 254, 288), for personal identity (I. 404), for visual experiences (II. 198), and so on. This is a varied list, and one in which linguistic expressions certainly do not predominate. If we think in terms of the criteria and standards to which we might refer everyday affairs, it seems as though we would use the criteria to determine whether someone has a certain opinion, whether a person is in a state of expectation, and so on. Among the above examples it is only where Wittgenstein speaks of "the criteria for 'fitting,' 'being able to,' and 'understanding'" (I. 182) that criteria have the appearance of governing linguistic expressions.

There are, indeed, other passages where Wittgenstein makes it appear that he takes criteria to govern, in some way, what is said. For example:

> The man who says "Only my pain is real," doesn't mean to say that he has found out by the common criteria—the criteria, i.e., which give our words their common meaning—that the others who said they had pains were cheating. But what he rebels against is the use of *this* expression in connection with *these* criteria. (*BBB*, p. 57)
>
> Suppose I explain various methods of projection to someone so that he may go on to apply them; let us ask ourselves when we should say that *the* method that I intend comes before his mind. Now clearly we accept two different kinds of criteria for this.... (*Inv.* I. 141)

But these examples remain a minority. The decisive weight in favor of this second point is exegetical. Assuming that Wittgenstein's use of 'criterion' is distinctive, we must look to its relation to other prominent ideas in his later work for the key to its distinctive features; and the intimacy of the concepts of *grammar* and *criterion* requires that Wittgensteinian criteria characteristically have their application in connection with linguistic expression. When Wittgenstein speaks, e.g., of the criteria for a person's reading, we must remember that this is a shorthand locution, that what the criteria govern is our use of such expressions as 'A is reading,' that what they determine is not the empirical fact whether A is reading but the "meaning" of 'A is reading,' and that they form part of the "grammar" of such expressions as 'A is reading.'

Note an ambiguity in speaking of the criteria for someone's doing such-and-such: what is meant is not a test by which we might determine whether X does such-and-such (where it is assumed that the meaning of 'X does such-and-such' is antecedently known); but rather the standard grammatical test according to which a sentence of the form 'X does such-and-such' is used, when it is used in a normal or correct way. The manager of a supermarket might explain to a new employee that the way of telling that a lug of fruit from California contains tomatoes rather than peaches is that the cover-paper is light blue rather than dark blue, the labels being identical; but although such a "way of telling" might properly be regarded as a criterion, it would not be a Wittgensteinian criterion. This ambiguity is adequately resolved when the context of the passages is preserved and Wittgenstein's logical theory kept in mind; it need not obscure the focus of the concept of a criterion—as it might do for someone who has the supermarket criterion for tomatoes in mind when he reads Norman Malcolm's statement that a criterion is "something that settles a question with certainty" (*D*, p. 60).

3. *The utterances for which there are criteria are those that make statements which the speaker has some way of knowing to be true or to be false, or which he might justify by reference to something other than what is stated in his utterance.* It is clear that *criterion* is a narrower concept than *grammar*: not every linguistic expression has a criterion, though every linguistic expression has a grammar. I cannot think, for example, what could be meant by "the criterion for 'Hello' "; and Wittgenstein explicitly says that there is no criterion of personal identity which makes it correct for me to say that "I" am in pain (*Inv.* I. 404), and again, that I do not identify my sensations by criteria (*Inv.* I. 290). It is therefore necessary to indicate *which* utterances have criteria—viz., those which have truth-conditions in the sense I have tried to express.

It might be noted in passing that we often speak of the criteria of such things as "fitting" or the concept of dreaming, and in such cases it superficially appears that it is something other than a statement to which the criterion applies. These locutions are best thought of as shorthand expressions for referring to the criterion or criteria which govern the use of any utterance with truth-conditions, in which the term in question appears as the main verb or in some equally prominent spot.

4. *All utterances of this sort have criteria governing their use.* A criterion is a standard—that is, an objective reference for ascertaining or checking something; and the standard is, of course, public. Once we agree that criteria govern the use of certain linguistic expressions, it is reasonable to expect that they govern the use of all those utterances that make statements which the speaker can know, justify, or verify. This expectation is borne out by the texts. Albritton finds this feature of criteria prominent in Wittgenstein's discussion in the *Blue Book*, where a symptom is explained as a phenomenon which we find through experience to coincide with a criterion: "If there is *no* criterion by which I might judge that I myself have a toothache, for example, then it will follow that nothing can be a symptom for me of my having one."[3] So anything for which there are symptoms must

---

[3] Rogers Albritton, "On Wittgenstein's Use of the Term 'Criterion'," *Journal of Philosophy*, LVI, 1959, p. 849.

have a criterion (or criteria). And since (*BBB*, pp. 24–25) we can only answer the question "How do you know that so-and-so is the case?" by giving criteria (a grammatical explanation) or symptoms (an empirical justification), it follows that I must have some criterion for any statement which I can *know* or *justify*. In the later work, strong textual support for this point comes from the fact that Wittgenstein feels justified, whenever considering a dark or dubious assertion, in asking what the criterion for it would be; this is, indeed, the predominant use of 'criterion' in the *Philosophical Investigations*.[4]

The last two points show an affinity between Wittgenstein's use of 'criterion' and the Verifiability Theory of Meaning. The similarity is that in both cases a statement is challenged or clarified by asking, in effect, what would show the statement to be true and what would show it to be false. This affinity finds its most open expression when Wittgenstein says: "Asking whether and how a proposition can be verified is only a particular way of asking 'How d'you mean?' The answer is a contribution to the grammar of the proposition" (*Inv.* I. 353). This congruity is worthy of note, for its historical as well as its philosophical interest; it brings out an important continuity between the earlier and the later Wittgenstein.

At the same time there are differences to be kept in mind. Most importantly, Wittgenstein appears to regard certain statements which are paradigms of verified utterances for the Verifiability Theory—basic or protocol sentences or avowals—as exempt from this logical test. Such statements have been said in the past to be the only ones fully verified. That these have no criteria, according to Wittgenstein, comes out most clearly in his discussion of pain. No one would argue that I must have a criterion whenever I cry out in pain; when Wittgenstein says that "the verbal expression of pain replaces crying" (*Inv.* I. 244), the inference suggests itself that 'I am in pain' and 'My foot is sore' do not have criteria either. As Malcolm has pointed out (*KOM*, p. 978), this comparison is surprising since no one would say that a cry of pain has a truth-value or a contradictory, whereas the *statement* that I am in pain has both. Wittgenstein, however, is not drawing a circle around what can be true or false (as do Verifiability Theorists), but around what can be known or justified. 'I am in pain' lies within the first circle but not the second: "It can't be said of me at all (except perhaps as a joke) that *I know* I am in pain. What is it supposed to mean—except perhaps that I *am* in pain?" (*Inv.* I. 246). And since the concept of a criterion applies to all that is within the known-or-justified circle, and to nothing outside it, my saying that I am in pain is exempt

---

[4] It occurs in the following passages: Part I, 160, 182, 190, 238, 239, 253, 322, 377, 385, 509, 572, 573, 625; and Part II on pages 185, 198, 211 and 222—almost half of the passages in which the term appears.

from such a standard (*Inv.* I. 290). Malcolm puts the point neatly: "One does not find out that one is in pain by employing a criterion. Indeed it makes no sense to speak of *finding out* that one is in pain, when this would imply that one was previously in pain but not aware of it. There is, however, a criterion for determining whether someone uses the sentence 'I am in pain' correctly—and this makes it an intelligible sentence" (*D*, p. 15).

This is a point at which Wittgenstein differs sharply from the Logical Positivists, while not directly contradicting them. The import of Wittgenstein's remarks for the Verifiability Theory is best thought of not as a repudiation of that theory but as a restriction of its application to statements which the speaker can know or justify.

5. *Criteria are always the criteria of some person or group of persons.* This feature should be evident from the mere fact that criteria are human instruments, and it is worth stressing chiefly because of the misunderstanding it can forestall—in particular that of confusing criteria with necessary and sufficient conditions. It would be absurd to suppose that for *you* the necessary and sufficient conditions for an acorn's growing into an oak might be different from what they are for *me*. The necessary and sufficient conditions for something are in the world, not in language or human conventions. With criteria the case is different, and there may be a divergence between your criterion for something and mine. Wittgenstein gives an instance of this when he considers what might be said if someone were to ask him whether he still knows what he was going to say when interrupted:

> If I do know now, and say it—does that mean that I had already thought it before, only not said it? No. Unless you take the certainty with which I continue the interrupted sentence as a criterion of the thought's already having been completed at that time. (*Inv.* I. 633)

I do not mean that whenever one talks about criteria one must *say* whose they are. It may sometimes prevent misunderstanding to use the personal possessive pronouns with 'criterion,' but much of the time this is not necessary. When Malcolm speaks of "the criterion of dreaming," it is clear enough that he is referring to the criterion which speakers of the language have in common, and which they all learn to use when they learn to tell their dreams. What is important is not any form of words, but rather that the human ancestry of criteria not be betrayed in the course of analysis, exposition or extrapolation of the concept—as it is when Michael Scriven, in what he takes to be the spirit of Wittgenstein, says that the criteria for something's being a lemon are certain *properties* of lemons, and speaks of them as being either "analytic" or "normic."[5]

6. *Criteria are arbitrary, in that there need be no justification for criteria being what they are.* At one point Wittgenstein supposes that I have explained that my criterion for another person's having a toothache is that he holds his cheek in a certain way. He goes on:

> Now one may go on and ask: "How do you know that he has got toothache when he holds his cheek?" The answer to this might be, "I say *he* has toothache when he holds his cheek because I hold my cheek when I have toothache." But what if we went on asking: —"And why do you suppose that [his] toothache corresponds to his holding his cheek just because your toothache corresponds to your holding your cheek?" You will be at a loss to answer this question, and find that here we strike rock bottom, that is we have come down to conventions. (*BBB*, p. 24)

The whole point of criteria is that they determine what we say; and so the question why, when we have some criterion or other, we say what the criterion determines we should say—this is a question which soon loses all point. We can consider a criterion as giving us a rule which indicates what we are to say. We do not have *reasons* for following such a rule as we do; we are rather trained to follow it when we learn the language.

> Let me ask this: what has the expression of a rule—say a signpost—got to do with my actions? What sort of connection is there here?—Well, perhaps this one: I have been trained to react to this sign in a particular way, and now I do so react to it. (*Inv.* I. 198)
> *We need have no reasons to follow the rule as we do.* The chain of reasons has an end. (*BBB*, p. 143)

I do not believe that Wittgenstein intends that we can never give reasons for having the criteria we do, but rather that we need not and ordinarily do not. In the special case of the technical language of the sciences, where theory plays a large role and precise neologisms are frequent, the justification of criteria is probably more common than in lay speech. A Wittgensteinian scientist of the 17th century might have said: "I know the word 'force' is not used with such narrow precision in ordinary parlance; but if we rigorously take only *ma* and not *mv* as our criterion for the force of an object, we can formulate a simpler and more coherent theory." The facilitation of theory has often served in the past, and can still serve today, as a kind of justification for the criteria of scientific expressions. Wittgen-

[5] "The Logic of Criteria," *Journal of Philosophy*, LVI, 1959, p. 861.

stein acknowledges as much when he says that "A reform for particular practical purposes, an improvement in our terminology designed to prevent misunderstandings in practice, is perfectly possible" (*Inv.* I. 132). Such justification occurs but rarely, however, with respect to the common language which we all learn as we grow up.

7. *To explain the criteria of X is to give a partial grammatical explanation of 'X.'* This statement generalizes a remark made by Wittgenstein (*BBB*, p. 24), and I have already argued for it. It is worth repeating here because the connection between criteria and grammar is at the root of the next few features which I shall have to state.

8. *There is no such thing as an inner or private criterion,* in the sense of a criterion which another person could not even be conceived to use. Albritton raises the question, "And is there no inner criterion for a toothache?" He apparently thinks it might be answered in the affirmative. I find this suggestion implausible in the extreme, and I take the fact that Albritton draws this possibility out of his reading of Wittgenstein's remarks, as a sign that his account of Wittgenstein's use of 'criterion' is inaccurate. A criterion, C, governs the use of a linguistic expression, 'P.' This means that if I know how to use 'P'—i.e., if I know how to apply C—I must be able to distinguish between a correct use of 'P' and a misuse of 'P.' If I have such a measure of correctness, it must be an objective one—otherwise it would be no measure—and therefore open to the view of anyone who cares to look and see. If my criterion for 'P' were a private one, completely inaccessible to anyone else, I could never, however strong my impression of being right, make any sense of a distinction between my *thinking* such-and-such a use of 'P' to be correct and that use's really *being* correct. Wittgenstein has pointed out that where there is no distinction between being right and thinking one is right there is no being right either: "In the present case I have no criterion of correctness. One would like to say: whatever is going to seem right to me is right. And that only means that here we can't talk about 'right' " (*Inv.* I. 258).

Without a distinction between a correct use and a misuse, the notion of a private criterion evaporates into absurdity. It is, indeed, subject to the full impact of Wittgenstein's argument against the possibility of private language.[6]

[6] *Inv.* I. 243–280, esp. 256–270. See also my paper, "Wittgenstein on Private Language," *Philosophy and Phenomenological Research,* XX, 1960, pp. 389–396; and Malcolm in *KOM,* pp. 975–976. It might be thought that Wittgenstein leaves room for the notion of an inner criterion when he says that "an inner process stands in need of outward criteria" (*Inv.* I. 580). I do not believe that this is the case. The preceding argument decisively eliminates the notion of a private criterion, and

9. *Criteria are often embedded in linguistic practice, and the people who use them may be quite unable to say what they are.* Even in lands where children are taught to formulate the grammar of the language, this training does not generally extend to the "grammar" with which Wittgenstein is concerned: long after school-children can handle the relevant expressions with perfect aptness, they still do not have any explicit idea what the truth-conditions for 'He has a toothache' are, nor that there are no criteria for my saying that I have one.

Although people do not ordinarily *know about* the criteria they use, they do *know how* to use them. Here we come upon the familiar and still dangerous fact that the sentence 'N knows the criteria for "P" ' is ambiguous, since 'know' can have the sense of either 'know how' or 'know that,' as Gilbert Ryle has put it. That the latter sort of knowledge of our common criteria is rare should not blind us to the fact that people make propositions at apt junctures, recognize good and bad evidence for them, teach their children to use the relevant sentence, and in general give every evidence of a sound practical knowledge of these criteria. Conversely the ubiquity of this practical knowledge should not lead us to expect to find any intellectual appreciation of the subtleties of criteria.

10. *Criteria are generally rough and imprecise; it is regular use and acknowledgement, rather than precision, which makes them satisfactory.* They are, of course, as precise as they need be for human communication, but our requirements are a far cry from the "crystalline purity" which Wittgenstein, following Frege, once imagined to characterize our discourse.

There are two related ways in which this roughness of criteria shows itself. The first is that what the criteria for 'P' determine is the *sort* of thing that would show 'P' to be true or false; and to say whether some set of present circumstances are of this sort or not requires discrimination that is not determined by the criteria and cannot be prescribed, but can be learned only through practice. "A person goes by a sign-post only in so far as there exists a regular use of sign-posts, a custom" (*Inv.* I. 198). "*We need have no reason to follow the rule as we do. The chain of reasons has an end*" (*BBB*, p.

---

the redundancy of the phrase 'outward criteria' must be set down to rhetoric. Or one might get the idea of an inner private criterion from *Inv.* I. 141, where Wittgenstein says that one kind of criterion which we clearly accept for our saying that the method of projection I intend comes before another person's mind is "the picture (of whatever kind) that comes before his mind." But if the picture coming before *his* mind is a criterion for us, it cannot be a *private* inner criterion; here we should remember that an "inner process" stands in need of outward criteria and cannot, under such circumstances, be regarded as "private."

143). Criteria are a part of the form of life which people have in common, and Wittgenstein offers little reason to believe that such forms of life might be precisely and exhaustively described.

The second way in which the roughness of criteria shows itself is in our inability to say exactly what the criteria are for even simple utterances. It is a noteworthy fact, apparent to anyone who reviews his use of 'criterion,' that Wittgenstein never gives a detailed description of any criteria; he says, indeed, that "in most cases we are unable to do so" (*BBB*, p. 25). An example may make it clear why this should be so, and why it is innocuous. A man puts a gun to his shoulder, a shot sounds, and a duck falls to the ground. We say that the man aimed at the duck and shot it. We may even say that *that* is just what we call aiming and shooting, and thereby indicate successfully the criterion for a man's aiming at and shooting something. But this does not mean that it is *certain* that the man did aim at the duck and shoot it. It may turn out that the man is blind, or that the gun was electronically rigged to aim itself, or that an accomplice did the shooting, or that there is no sign of a wound on the bird. If any of these further circumstances should obtain, the claim would have to be withdrawn or in some way qualified—although we might still correctly say that that is the sort of thing we ordinarily call aiming at and shooting a duck. The number of possible exceptions to 'P' may be infinite, but my failure to specify them does not entail that I fail to indicate the criteria for 'P.'

11. *Criteria presuppose circumstances of application.* This feature is particularly apparent in cases where there are many different criteria for something, rather than one defining criterion. Albritton emphasizes this aspect of Wittgenstein's use of 'criterion,' and it may be illustrated by the following passages:

> Now it cannot be doubted that we regard certain facial expressions, gestures, etc., as characteristic for the expression of belief. We speak of a 'tone of conviction.' And yet it is clear that this tone of conviction isn't always present whenever we rightly speak of conviction. "Just so," you might say, "this shows that there is something else, something behind these gestures etc., which is the real belief as opposed to mere expressions of belief."—"Not at all," I should say, "many different criteria distinguish, under different circumstances, cases of believing what you say from those of not believing what you say." (*BBB*, p. 144)

> In different circumstances we apply different criteria for a person's reading. (*Inv.* I. 164)

In these cases we might say that the criteria are complementary, in the sense in which the different phonetic criteria of the English phoneme /p/ are complementary.

The vast majority of common concepts have several complementary criteria rather than a single defining criterion. There are exceptions among scientific concepts; it may even be an ideal of science that each of its concepts should have only a single defining criterion, and to the extent that scientific theory aims at enunciating propositions that are true in *all* circumstances, this ideal is readily understandable. But even in science the concepts with a single defining criterion are by and large limited to sections of scientific thought where there is a single universally recognized theory, and if one examines concepts in the vanguard of scientific advance— the concept of force in the sixteenth and seventeenth centuries or that of a chemical element in the nineteenth—one sees different criteria competing against or complementing one another. Whatever the case may be with science, ordinary assertions have a more limited use, bounded by the circumstances in which they are made; and their criteria need not be identical with the criteria of the same utterances in different circumstances.

12. *There may be a fluctuation between the criteria of something and the symptoms of it.* In *Inv.* I. 79 Wittgenstein takes note of this fluctuation in the case of scientific definitions: "What counts today as an observed concomitant of a phenomenon will tomorrow be used to define it"; and in *Inv.* I. 354 he says that "the fluctuation in grammar between criteria and symptoms makes it look as if there were nothing at all but symptoms." The supposition that in such cases there are only symptoms must certainly be illusory, for it is incompatible with the requirement that I must have a criterion for every statement which I can justify or *know* to be true; but the fluctuation is real enough. The previous point has prepared us for finding different criteria for something in different circumstances; but we might have thought that what counted as criterion in one context could not count as symptom in another, and *vice versa*. Taking note of the fluctuation between criteria and symptoms makes it clear that the variation can be of the latter sort as well.

It is not hard to point to examples of this sort of fluctuation, and Wittgenstein has not been the only one to observe it. It is common for criteria and symptoms of something's having the temperature 0° C. to be interchanged. On one occasion I may explain that thermometers are designed to indicate the temperature at which pure water freezes under a certain atmospheric pressure; here I take the change of state of pure water as my criterion for the temperature being 0° C., and the behaviour of thermometers as a symptom, that is, "a phenomenon of which experience has taught us that it coincided, in some way or other, with the phenomenon which is our defining criterion" (*BBB*, p. 25). On another occasion I may regard thermometers as having unquestioned authority, and state that the change of state of pure water at sea-level is correlated (as a symptom) with the temperature being 0° C.; and here the former symptom is my criterion, and my former criterion a symptom. This sort of fluctuation also occurs with the term 'force': either the formula '$F = k\varDelta l$' or the formula '$F = ma$' can be taken as expressing the criterion of force; whichever formula is taken as giving the criterion, the other will in that context express the correlation of a certain phenomenon with this criterion. Two points about such fluctuation deserve to be noticed. First, it might also be described as a fluctuation between the "grammatical" and the "empirical" use of the same expression (cf. *Inv.* I. 251). The sentence 'Water freezes at 0° C.' and the formula '$F = ma$' have a "grammatical" use when they express the speaker's criteria; otherwise they have an "empirical" use. Secondly, such fluctuation occurs only where there is a reliable correlation between phenomena, such as obtains in scientific matters or between the visual and the kinaesthetic criteria for touching my nose. Thus such fluctuation is common in scientific discourse because of what Feigl calls "the essentially network-like character of scientific theories."

The fluctuation between criteria and symptoms is conditioned by the contextual character of criteria. A conversation ordinarily has a certain aim and certain presuppositions, and the criteria must be among the presuppositions. They may be explained in grammatical propositions; but these explanations do not in themselves constitute progress toward the aim of the conversation—they make for progress only in the sense in which putting an edge on a scythe helps to mow grass, and thus, in Kant's terms, they are explicative rather than ampliative. Not all conversations have the same presuppositions or the same aim, and the same sentence which expresses a grammatical explanation in one context may express an empirical proposition in another—i.e., the criteria may become symptoms. What cannot be permitted, by Wittgenstein or anyone else, is that phenomena should *in the same context* count as both criteria and symptoms, nor that a proposition should be *simultaneously* both explicative and ampliative. But when we take cognizance of the fact that criteria are contextually conditioned, and do not attach irrevocably to terms or concepts, then we can see how the same concept may have sometimes one and sometimes another criterion. Since different criteria may be criteria for the same concept, a fluctuation between criteria and symptoms is not necessarily a sign of ambiguity, and does not "destroy logic"—as it would do if it meant that there were only symptoms.

13. *Criteria can "coincide" or "conflict."* We may begin by noting that the cases where one speaks of the coincidence or conflict of criteria are ones in which two or more sorts of phenomena regularly occur together: Wittgenstein speaks, for example, of the coincidence of the "many different criteria" (he mentions four) that a man may have for his pointing to his own eye (*BBB*, pp. 63–64). It is in the light of this fact that we can see most easily what is meant by saying that criteria coincide. The criteria which a man may have for pointing to his eye, according to Wittgenstein's account, include (1) the kinaesthetic experience of raising his arm to his eyes, (2) the tactile sensation of his finger touching his eye, (3) the visual experience of his finger appearing before his eye, and (4) the visual experience of seeing (in a mirror or a TV screen) his finger in the appropriate relation to his eye. He then says: "If these criteria, as they usually do, coincide, I may use them alternately and in different circumstances. . . ." I take it, then, that what it means to say that the criteria for 'P' coincide, is simply that the various phenomena, each of which is commonly (or sometimes) used as a criterion for 'P' in particular circumstances, are invariably associated (or very nearly so).

A "conflict" of criteria is more difficult to understand. The sense in which Wittgenstein's remarks about the concept of a man pointing to his eye seem to leave room for a conflict of criteria is that the criteria need not coincide—that is, the phenomena which are commonly regarded as criteria, and which as a matter of fact are invariably associated (or nearly so), might *conceivably not* occur in such regular conjunction with one another. If this explanation is correct, it gives a sense to the expression 'possible conflict of criteria.' But could there be in some sense an *actual* conflict among the various criteria of the *same* concept? To answer this question we shall have to examine what would happen if the various phenomena which we find in conjunction should cease to occur together.

In discussing another example Wittgenstein says:

> The *ordinary* use of the word 'person' is what one might call a composite use suitable under the ordinary circumstances. If I assume, as I do, that these circumstances are changed, the application of the term 'person' or 'personality' has thereby changed; and if I wish to preserve this term and give it a use analogous to its former use, I am at liberty to choose between many uses, thinking between many different kinds of analogy. One might say in such a case that the term 'personality' hasn't got one legitimate heir only. (*BBB*, p. 62)

If our criteria cease to coincide, the concept as we know it breaks apart, and the expression in question no longer has *any* clear use.

Consequently it is very difficult to see what sense there would be in continuing to give the name 'criteria' to those phenomena which used to count as criteria; and without criteria there could, of course, be no conflict of criteria.

We arrive, then, at the seemingly paradoxical position that criteria which in fact coincide might possibly conflict, but that there could not be an actual conflict among the various criteria of a single concept. There is, of course, no inconsistency in this position, and I think it sheds a useful light on Wittgenstein's use of 'criterion.' The apparent paradox disappears when we bear in mind that criteria are human instruments with characteristic uses, that their application presupposes circumstances which do more or less frequently obtain, and that where these circumstances do not obtain our criteria do not apply and thus, for all practical purposes, cease to exist.

Postscript

I have so far tried to be straightforwardly exegetical in my examination of the concept of a criterion. In conclusion I wish to be somewhat more polemical, and to make clear that I regard some of the important things Albritton and Malcolm have said about criteria as incompatible with the exegesis I have set forth.

Albritton and I differ in viewpoint. Rather than approach the exegesis of the concept *criterion* on the basis of its affinity with the concept *grammar*, he begins by considering the expression 'defining criterion,' which he takes to denote some sort of necessary and sufficient condition. Thus a criterion of X is some sort of a condition for X's being so, and Albritton's exegetical problem is to determine *what* sort of condition. But to begin in this manner is to set off in the wrong direction. The terminology is alien and inimical to Wittgenstein's thought, for the concept of a criterion was introduced by Wittgenstein precisely to avoid speaking of necessary and sufficient conditions with respect to those logical relations where such a formal notion does not apply. Criteria are human instruments, whereas conditions are natural phenomena; criteria are used or applied, whereas conditions obtain; criteria are arbitrary or conventional, and when we reach them "the chain of reasons has an end," whereas statements about necessary and sufficient conditions are justified by something else, generally by scientific laws; conditions are conceptually independent of what they are conditions for, whereas criteria (in Wittgenstein's sense) are not; and so on. Only confusion and perplexity can result from amalgamating two such diverse concepts; and although Albritton's paper has substantial merits, I cannot help but conclude that he goes astray at the very beginning by viewing Wittgenstein's logical theory from the wrong perspective.

Malcolm, if my exegesis has been sound, departs from Wittgenstein in two important respects. The first is his blurring of the distinction between criteria and evidence. He says that a criterion "settles a question with certainty" (*D*, p. 60), and that "the application of a criterion must be able to yield either an affirmative or a negative result" (*D*, p. 24). At another point he says: "If he [Mill] had a criterion he could apply it, establishing with certainty that this or that human figure does or does not have feeling. . . ." (*KOM*, p. 970). I take it that Malcolm's remarks apply to questions about how it is with the world, not just to questions about how a linguistic expression is to be used. To answer questions of this sort Wittgenstein insists that we must refer to "symptoms" or evidence; in maintaining that we can answer such questions "with certainty" by reference to criteria Malcolm erases the distinction (which Wittgenstein was careful to preserve) between the truth-conditions and the truth-value of a proposition, between meaning and truth —and thus he threatens the foundations of logic.

Malcolm's second departure from Wittgenstein occurs in his implicit denial of "the fluctuation of scientific definitions" (*Inv.* I. 79) which occurs when scientists elaborate new criteria to coincide with the original ones. The whole burden of his attack on Dement and Kleitman (*D*, ch. 13) rests upon his charge that they adopt physiological phenomena (REM periods and EEG patterns) as a criterion of dreaming, and the principal "error" with which he taxes them is that of not "holding firmly to waking testimony as the sole criterion of dreaming" (*D*, p. 81). Finding a new coinciding criterion for a phenomenon under investigation is one of the legitimate and useful aims of a scientist, and to go along with Malcolm's second departure from Wittgenstein would be to take up a form of linguistic Romanticism and to place an unwarranted shackle on scientific progress. Malcolm appears, therefore, to have erred twice in the details of Wittgenstein's logical theory, and to have slipped into logical confusion which Wittgenstein himself avoided.

COMMENTS

CARL GINET

I share with Mr. Garver two opinions that seem to underlie his paper. First, we think that Wittgenstein's later views on the nature of logical truth are essentially sound and philosophically very helpful. Second, we believe that the nature of criteria needs systematic explanation, clarification, even elaboration, if the use that Wittgenstein and other philosophers make of this notion is to be clearly understood and freed from puzzlement and suspicion.

I think, however, that Mr. Garver's efforts to fill this need are not entirely satisfactory, even as far as they go. So I propose to discuss several points on which I think his discussion is inadequate, confused, or simply mistaken.

First, however, I must express my agreement with his important point that it makes sense to speak of the criterion for the application of a given term to a thing only where it would also make sense to speak of those applying it to that thing as coming to know that, or as having weak grounds for believing that, or as being ignorant that, the term applies to the thing. And I agree that this sort of talk does not make sense with regard to one's applying terms like 'pain' to one's own mental states.

My main complaint about Garver's discussion concerns his treatment of the relation between criteria and necessary and sufficient conditions. I find baffling the ways in which, in his discussion of Albritton, he contrasts the two:

> Criteria are human instruments, whereas conditions are natural phenomena; criteria are used or applied, whereas conditions obtain; criteria are arbitrary or conventional, and when we reach them "the chain of reasons" has an end, whereas statements about necessary and sufficient conditions are justified by something else, generally by scientific laws; conditions are conceptually independent of what they are conditions for, whereas criteria . . . are not.

My puzzlement here is only with what is said on the side of conditions. Would Mr. Garver deny that there are *defining* conditions or *logically* necessary and sufficient ones? Can we not say that these are *used* in the application of terms in just the way that Garver wants to say that criteria are used? Surely no one has ever thought of explaining the notion of criteria in terms of necessary and sufficient conditions of any other sort. Yet Garver, if his remarks are true, is speaking of conditions of quite another sort—those that are sometimes called *contingent* or *empirical*. Thus he leaves the question of the relation of criteria to *defining* necessary and sufficient conditions completely untouched. This is unfortunate because the feeling that criteria are somehow suspect very often arises, I believe, from wondering how precisely they are both like and yet not the same as necessary and sufficient defining conditions.

Wittgenstein's notion of a criterion is a *generalization* of the notion of a defining necessary and sufficient condition. The need for a more general notion of defining conditions, which does not require that they be blessed with necessity or sufficiency and which yet distinguishes them from other sorts of grounds for applying terms to things, is part of the radical shift in Wittgenstein's view about the nature of *all* logical truth. I mean the shift from the idea that *all* meanings, *all* correct applications of concepts, *all* logical relationships among terms, are determined by the eternally fixed objects-in-logical-space, something absolutely rigid and absolutely sharp in its boundaries, to the idea that all these things are determined by the more fluid, worldly things of human custom and agreement in human responses (which *can*, but do not necessarily, have great precision, rigidity, and force). It is only through appreciating the implications of this human-practice conception of *all* logical truth that the inadequacies of the necessary and sufficient defining condition and the need for a more general notion in handling intractable concepts will be brought home to anyone.

What, within the whole field of grounds, or reasons, for applying a term to a thing, marks the distinction between those that are to be called criteria and the others, which Wittgenstein calls "symptoms"?[1] Garver cites Wittgenstein's explanation of this distinction but does not note that according to it one species of criteria, or defining conditions, can be necessary and sufficient ones. A property is taken, or used, as a ground for applying a term to a thing either (1) because it has been associated in experience with another property, or (2) because it is the convention or practice of the users of the language to take that property as a ground for applying that term. It is the latter sort of ground that is to be called a criterion, and the former, a symptom.[2]

[1] It seems to me that the *criterion* for applying a given term on a given occasion should mean the *whole* ground, of the sort to be specified, for applying it on that occasion; a part only of the whole criteriological ground should be referred to as a part of the criterion and *not* as "one of the criteria."

[2] What Garver says about Malcolm's blurring the distinction between criteria and symptoms strikes me as wrong, and not consistent with his other criticism of Malcolm for which there does seem to be some foundation. In his discussion of dreaming Malcolm does seem to insist too firmly on the sharpness and fixity of the line between criteria and symptoms.

What needs to be said about this notion of a criterion, so defined, is not what Garver says, that it is a completely different notion from that of a rigorous definition and must be approached from a perspective completely different from that appropriate to rigorous definition. Rather it is that this notion has behind it a new perspective on the whole logical scene, including the precise, rigorously definable concepts of mathematics and science as well as more workaday ones.

So what needs explaining is how there can be involved in our linguistic practices criteria that *depart from* the model of the necessary and sufficient criterion in two ways: *first*, in not being the only criteria for the application of the associated terms, so that they are not logically necessary for that application and so that no conjunctions of conditions that are logically necessary are criteria; and *second*, in not being *logically sufficient* grounds for the application of the associated terms.

There are cases where one may speak of a term's signifying the same concept even though the criterion for its correct application is different upon different occasions. Garver alludes to this phenomenon in several places, but not in such a way as to throw much light on how it is possible. There are, in fact, several ways in which it can happen. One of these Garver seems to be trying to explain under his heading "*Criteria presuppose circumstances of application*" where he quotes Wittgenstein: "In different circumstances we apply different criteria for a person's reading." Garver speaks of *complementary* criteria, and gives the example of different sounds counting as utterances of the same English phoneme. The example is a valuable one, but I do not think that Garver has correctly interpreted Wittgenstein's remark. The different criteria we use in the different circumstances do not *presuppose* the different circumstances but *include* them. Garver's interpretation of the remark makes unnecessarily complicated the explanation of this phenomenon of a single concept with different criteria.

One thing that brings about the phenomenon is our natural propensity to see in a number of cases a sort of similarity that is not susceptible to analysis in terms of elements exactly the same in all the cases. And one account of how *this* happens is by means of the family-resemblance idea: It seems natural to group a number of cases together when they can be arranged in a series such that any two adjacent members are grouped together because of striking and clear similarities and each of these is grouped with its other neighbor because of a somewhat different but overlapping set of similarities, and so on indefinitely until two members remote from each other may have no important similarities at all.

But this family-resemblance explanation will not work for other cases where we see a similarity that cannot be analyzed in terms of elements exactly the same. Consider, for example, different shades of red; Garver's different soundings of the same phoneme; the different applications of such a word as 'broken' in 'broken glass,' 'broken watch,' 'broken promise,' 'broken spirit'; and different applications of an aesthetic term such as 'delicate.' In such cases (on which Wittgenstein places some emphasis in the *Blue Book*) all we can say is that we do see the cases as similar. We do see one as calling for the same term we customarily apply to another. This is what we do. There need be no further explanation, no further reason we have that analysis can reveal—to apply a remark of Garver's to a situation that gives it some point. Our doing so is thus in a sense arbitrary, as Garver indicates, but not in the sense that it is the result of an arbitrary *decision*. For it may be a matter of the most irresistible natural inclination—an important point that Garver fails to make clear.

Garver alludes to still another explanation of this phenomenon of complementary criteria when he talks of the shifting from symptoms to criteria. But he speaks as though there might be a shift back the other way, from criterion to symptom, and indeed many shiftings back and forth from occasion to occasion of the term's use; I do not see how this can happen with a univocal term. What I can understand is this: a ground, A, is first a symptom, taken as a ground only because it is correlated with something else, B, that is a criterion, but then A acquires the status of a criterion when as a result of sufficient use, it is no longer regarded as perfectly sensible and straightforward to say that the term would apply to a case where B was present but A was not, or to say that the term would *not* apply to a case where A was present but B was not. In all such cases (including Garver's examples, sec. 12)—where it is believed that two properties are always associated (also including those where both properties have an equally long history as criteria), where now one, now the other, is treated as the whole criteriological ground for the application of the concept, and (most important) where there is general puzzlement as to whether the term applies in hypothetical cases in which one or the other property is imagined absent—we should speak, not of a shifting back and forth from symptom to criterion, but simply of two criteria for the same term. And we should say that the use of both for the negative and positive application of that term is founded on a belief or presumption that they are universally associated. This is why the use leaves us baffled, gives no decision, where the presupposition is taken as false.

The other possibility that I said needed clear explanation was that of a criterion that is not a logically sufficient condition. This possibility is illustrated by Garver's example of the criterion for saying of a man that he aimed and shot at a duck, but Garver seems unclear about what his example illustrates. He introduces it as an example of the impossibility of specifying a criterion *completely* since the criteriological ground that can be indicated does not make it certain (leaving no room for doubt) that the man was aiming and shooting; thus he appears to assume that a *complete* specification of a criterion has to make it logically sufficient. Yet he closes his discussion of this example with the thought that one's inability to specify all the exceptional circumstances that might, in spite of the presence of what one ordinarily calls aiming and shooting, falsify the description, 'aiming and shooting,' does not show that one is unable to indicate the criterion (what is *ordinarily* called aiming and shooting); thus he appears to imply that what one *can* indicate is a criterion even though it is not logically sufficient.

This possibility of a logically insufficient criterion is indeed a difficult one, and I must confess that I do not like it. I have heard it suggested that insufficiency characterizes all our criteria for applying psychological predicates to others; I would hope that it is not so. But I see no way of denying that there may be some predicates (e.g., those ascribing complex intentions to persons) for which our criteria are not, and cannot be, logically sufficient. There do seem to be cases where every criterion actually used for a term, is such that it is possible to imagine the criterion surrounded with unusual circumstances that would properly make the users withdraw the term even though this possibility would not normally be a reasonable ground for genuine doubt. One may be inclined to think that in such cases the sufficiency of the criterion could be preserved by saying that it really *includes* the absence of all such unusual surroundings. But the difficulty is in giving definite content to the phrase 'all such unusual surroundings.' For it is possible that there may not be any known definite variety of them, or any way of stating or imagining what makes any new surrounding count as nullifying the application of the term in spite of the positive criterion. What marks the sort of surrounding that nullifies the criterion may be the sort of (so-called) similarity we mentioned before, which we can *see* when the cases are before the mind but cannot explain in terms of common elements exactly the same. If so, then we are forced to admit that it is impossible to display or state (except in synonymous terms) any criterion that is logically sufficient.

Such insufficient criteria might (to combine two familiar pieces of jargon) be said to possess "open-ended defeasibility." This name would at least have the merit of suggesting that the trait is not, as Mr. Garver seems to think, easy to understand.

COMMENTS

F. A. SIEGLER

1. Has Wittgenstein a logical theory? He disavows having any sort of theory at all. A doctor who makes a claim about having measles should be taken seriously in his claim; and similarly the fact that Wittgenstein disavows any logical theory should lead one carefully to question assertions that he does have one. Now Mr. Garver does not state what Wittgenstein's logical theory is, nor does he *show* that Wittgenstein has one. But he does constantly say that Wittgenstein has one. It is therefore reasonable to wonder what theory is attributed to him, and what are the grounds for saying that he has it.

2. What is a criterion? Mr. Garver says many different things:

a. Criteria govern the meaning of 'A is reading' (p. 59).
b. "We refer to criteria in order to decide about the propriety of an utterance or argument or . . . inference" (p. 57).
c. "The whole point of criteria is that they determine what we say . . . what we should say . . . what we are to say" (p. 63).
d. The criterion provides a distinction between a correct and an incorrect use of a linguistic expression (p. 64).
e. It is by a criterion that I justify a statement or know it to be true (pp. 60–62).

All these remarks may be connected but it is not clear from what Mr. Garver says what is the connection he may mean. By 'criteria' Mr. Garver seems to have at least three different sorts of things in mind: (1) what determines the meaning of a linguistic expression (as in *a*); (2) conventions for using a linguistic expression correctly (as in *b–d*); (3) conventions which determine when one is justified in claiming to know that something is the case (as in *e*).

I suppose that most linguistic expressions have meanings although it is not clear what 'Hello' means. When two people meet, 'Hello' is not generally said after other words but before, if at all. I suppose this to be a convention for the use of the linguistic expression 'Hello.' Yet in his introductory remarks Mr. Garver says, "In the place of the mathematical precision of formal logic Wittgenstein emphasizes grammar, which rests upon agreement in the way people act, upon a form of life" (p. 56).

Mr. Garver says that "the utterances for which there are criteria are those that make statements for which the person uttering them has some way of knowing them to be true or to be false, or which he might justify by reference to something other than what is stated in his utterance" (p. 60). Now this conflicts with Mr. Garver's sense (2) because there are criteria in sense (2) for 'Get out' and 'Help.' Perhaps Mr. Garver means criteria in sense (3). Yet he often speaks as though he means criteria in sense (2). He says (agreeing with Malcolm) "there is a criterion for determining whether someone uses the sentence 'I am in pain' correctly—and this makes it an intelligible sentence" (p. 62). This implies that unless a linguistic expression (sentence) has a criterion for determining its correct use it is unintelligible. But he also appears to hold, with Wittgenstein, that there are utterances for which a speaker does not require a criterion and which yet are meaningful (see his section 3).

3. Usually, the suggestion is that we employ criteria although we do not have explicit knowledge of what the criteria are. When *do* we speak of employing criteria? When judging pigs and the like, of course. Perhaps when a doctor is trying to decide whether a patient has a particularly rare disease, he might be said to employ criteria. But does the doctor employ criteria in telling his nurse that the patient smelled of onions? In telling her that the patient is gone? The initial picture of employing a criterion is of checking up on some difficult or disputed issue. This matches a common context in which Wittgenstein uses the word 'criterion.' Does it follow from the fact that we employ criteria in certain difficult issues that we employ criteria when there is no dispute or problem about getting something right? That we deliberate on some issue does not imply that we deliberate on all issues before acting. Nor may we infer that our actions are always guided by deliberations.

4. "Criteria are human instruments." Are they instruments in a usual sense, or instead in some esoteric sense? I suppose that there is nothing lost in saying that a criterion is an instrument fashioned out of phenomena or circumstances, along side of scalpels and geiger counters. But then you have to spend so much time correcting false impressions. The same holds for Mr. Garver's characterization of criteria as "human contrivances." Tools, implements, apparatuses, etc. One begins to see that criteria are devices, inventions, part of a dark and deep human plot hatched expressly so that we can talk to each other.

5. Let me now offer some positive remarks on the notion of a criterion. It is rare to find a word which is applied on the basis of a set of necessary and sufficient conditions. We could cite 'triangle'

in Euclidean Geometry, but not elsewhere, e.g., in the first grade of school. Then in medicine perhaps 'angina' or in law 'minor' or 'adult' might be used in accordance with necessary and sufficient conditions. These words are technical and have a restricted use for specified purposes. Wittgenstein sees that such technical words are of importance for set purposes. But most words are not used on the basis of such criteria. And this does not mean that they are vague or arbitrary. It is just that aside from trivial explanations such as "The word 'game' applies to games or instances of gamehood," most words cannot be analyzed in terms of necessary and sufficient conditions.

Often Wittgenstein uses the notion of a criterion to avoid the suggestion of necessary and sufficient conditions. And the term is most often used in criticism of sceptical or metaphysical theses. And here the question is not "What are the necessary and sufficient conditions for something's being an X?" He asks the sceptic to explain in whatever way he likes what he means, or how he can mean what he must in order to say what he wishes to say, or how he can do what he implies he can do, or the like (e.g., *Inv.* I. 258). The questions asked to the holder of the private-language thesis are, "What is the criterion for the correctness of a claim about, or reference to, or description of, or identification of the private sensation E?" Wittgenstein is requesting that the holder of the private-language thesis explain the meaning of 'E' and its role in a language. If 'E' has no meaning and none of the other characteristic features of a word in a language then the thesis cannot be accepted.

In this argument the word 'criterion' is used along with 'understanding,' 'definition,' 'justification,' 'ostensive definition,' 'the technique of using a word.' Trying to find out what exactly is meant by these words involves trying to find out what the argument hopes to reveal. And this is, that the holder of the private-language thesis cannot explain how 'E' has a use in any language. For he cannot show that 'E' has a role similar to that of words in what is called "language."

Wittgenstein might have asked: what is the *evidence* that a man who claims to report the sensation E *again*, is making a correct claim? Wittgenstein sometimes seems to use the word 'criterion' to mean 'evidence' (e.g., early in *Inv.* I. 269). But this should be no great confusion. After all for Wittgenstein's purposes what difference does it make to ask for the criteria for something, or to ask whether in a *given* example or case there is any evidence which could *fulfil* the criteria (whatever they may be) for something? If there are criteria then *a fortiori* there could be evidence in particular cases; and if there is evidence in an imagined case then there are criteria.

There are probably many ways in which Wittgenstein uses the word. But even if I were persistent enough to find out all the ways in which he uses the word 'criterion' I should find out no more than I should, were I to find out that the scalpel is a tool used by medical men in operating on the body for the purpose of cutting something or other. That kind of knowing is the sort of thing that Aristotle says will not be of much help in first aid; and if Wittgenstein is of any help he should be helpful in philosophical first aid.

COMMENTS

PAUL ZIFF

Mr. Garver is concerned to explain what Wittgenstein meant by the word 'criterion.' He supposes that Wittgenstein presented a logical theory and that the concept of a criterion is of some importance in that theory.

I wish to raise two distinct objections to Mr. Garver's exegesis. First, I suggest that it is based on a misunderstanding of Wittgenstein's remarks. Secondly, even if it were not, it would be of doubtful help since it is consistently unclear and yet, I think, clearly inconsistent. I shall discuss the second objection first.

1. Mr. Garver says many things about the concept of a criterion. First and foremost, he stresses its connection with the concept of grammar. Unfortunately he fails to tell us what he means by the word 'grammar.' This would not be a difficulty were it not for the fact that his remarks make it quite clear that he, like Wittgenstein, is not talking about grammar in any literal sense of the word.

For example, Mr. Garver says that "The distinctive features of Wittgensteinian criteria are best set out in a series of 'grammatical propositions' about criteria." He goes on to say, "Criteria are human instruments." I take it the sentence 'Criteria are human instruments,' is supposed to express a "grammatical proposition about criteria." But what he means, I do not see. I should have thought that a statement to the effect that the word 'criteria' is a plural noun could reasonably be classed as a grammatical statement about 'criteria.' But of course that would be a grammatical statement not about criteria but about the word 'criteria.' Mr. Garver says that the statement that criteria are human instruments might be used as a grammatical explanation of the word 'criterion.' If by 'grammatical explanation' Mr. Garver actually meant grammatical explanation, what he is saying would be obviously false.

2. Mr. Garver says some puzzling things about criteria. He says they are human instruments; they are generally rough and imprecise; they are often embedded in linguistic practice; they have a purpose and they are applied under appropriate circumstances. I am inclined to suppose that a rough, imprecise human instrument embedded in linguistic practice is assuredly an *unding*. Criteria are not literally instruments, either human or otherwise. No doubt

Mr. Garver is not speaking literally. I believe it might help if he would do so.

3. Mr. Garver says that "the utterances for which there are criteria are those that make statements which the speaker has some way of knowing to be true or to be false, or which he might justify by reference to something other than what is stated in his utterance." But suppose I say, "There are human beings just like us living on a planet in some distant galactic system." I have no way of knowing whether or not that is true nor can I justify it. Does it follow that there are no criteria for the utterance in question? Or again, I have no way of knowing whether or not there will be a full-scale atomic war. Does it follow that there are no criteria for the utterance 'There will be a full-scale atomic war?'

4. To make matters worse, Mr. Garver's view here leads to contradiction. For suppose the utterance U is such that George has no way of knowing whether or not the statement he makes in uttering U is either true or false, but I have a way of knowing whether or not the statement made in uttering U is true. Then there both are and are not criteria for U. For example, even though I have no way of knowing whether or not there will be a full-scale atomic war, Mr. Khrushchev might know.

Mr. Garver could avoid this difficulty by adopting the heroic course of restricting his remarks to utterance tokens. But this would have curious consequences which I shall not bother to spell out.

I am inclined to suppose that Mr. Garver must be talking not about utterance tokens but about utterance types, for since utterance tokens occur uniquely, there would be little point in formulating criteria exclusively for tokens. And perhaps the utterance types that Mr. Garver is concerned with are those that, perhaps under appropriate grammatical transformation, can occur in the linguistic environment 'I know that. . . .' Such a view, however, at once poses the problem of what can be meant by the phrase 'those utterances that can occur in such an environment.'

Mr. Garver evidently wants to say there are no criteria for the utterance type 'I am in pain,' this presumably on the grounds that there is something wrong with the utterance 'I know that I am in pain.' Grammatically speaking—and I mean "grammatically"— there is nothing wrong with such an utterance. Semantically speaking, there is nothing deviant about the utterance. For example, suppose someone somehow hasn't learned to use the word 'pain' and doesn't know what pain is. If I ask him "Are you in pain?" he might reply "I haven't the slightest idea, that's not a word I have yet learned to use." Even so, he might be in pain, in which case he would be in pain and not know it. Suppose later he learns to use the word. I ask the same question and he replies "I am in pain." I say "Are you sure?" wondering whether he really has learned what pain is, and he replies "I know that I am in pain." If there is anything perplexing about all this I fail to see what it is. And Mr. Garver is surely in error if he supposes that Wittgenstein would object to what I have just been saying (cf. *Inv.* I. 288).

5. Mr. Garver says that "we often speak of the criteria of such things as 'fitting' or the concept of dreaming. . . ." He says that our locutions are best thought of "as shorthand expressions for referring to the criterion or criteria which govern the use of any utterance with truth-conditions, in which the term in question appears as the main verb or in some equally prominent spot." It follows from this that there are criteria for 'I dreamt that p' given that there are criteria for the concept of dreaming. But Mr. Garver explicitly states that there are no criteria for 'I dreamt that p.' Perhaps instead of "any" utterance, Mr. Garver simply meant "some." Thus when he speaks of the criteria for the concept of dreaming he means to be speaking of the criteria which govern the use of not any but only some sentences in which the word 'dream' occurs. But if so, it seems quite odd to speak of criteria for the concept of dreaming. Indeed, I fail to understand his use of the word 'concept.' If there are criteria for only some sentences in which the word 'dream' appears but not for others, do these different occurrences of the word 'dream' differ in meaning, are they to be associated with different concepts, or not?

6. I should now like to turn to my first objection, viz., that Mr. Garver's exegesis of Wittgenstein is based on a misunderstanding. I'm afraid that it is radically in error.

Unlike Mr. Garver, I see no reason to ignore or to discount Wittgenstein's own words. Nor do I see any reason to base an account of what Wittgenstein meant in what Malcolm says. Mr. Garver often speaks of "Wittgenstein's logical theory." To put the point bluntly, Wittgenstein doesn't have a logical theory, and if he had one, the place to look for it would be either in the *Tractatus* or in the *Remarks on the Foundations of Mathematics*. (Incidentally, the word 'criterion' is scarcely to be found in either of these works.) Wittgenstein was not concerned with theories.

Wittgenstein says: ". . . And we may not advance any kind of theory. There must not be anything hypothetical in our considerations. We must do away with all *explanation*, and description alone must take its place. And this description gets its light—i.e., its purpose—from the philosophical problems. These are, of course, not empirical problems; they are solved, rather, by looking into the workings of our language, and that in such a way as to make us recognize those workings: *in spite of* an urge to misunderstand them. The problems are solved, not by giving new information, but by arranging what we have always known. Philosophy is a battle against the bewitchment of our intelligence by means of language" (109). There is no reason to ignore these remarks of Wittgenstein. He surely meant what he said. It is repeated often enough, in various ways. Thus he says "If one tried to advance *theses* in philosophy, it would never be possible to question them, because everyone would agree to them" (128). "The work of the philosopher consists in assembling reminders for a particular purpose" (127). "The philosopher's treatment of a question is like the treatment of an illness" (255).

To put the matter plainly, it is not possible to refute Wittgenstein because there is nothing to refute. He makes no claims, he advances no theses. In particular, he has no theory of criteria.

7. Wittgenstein said of himself that he was doing philosophy in a new way, that his was a new sort of philosophy. He was, I believe, right in so saying.

Wittgenstein was concerned with philosophical problems and everything he said was in relation to some such problem. He says "The concept of a perspicuous representation is of fundamental significance for us. It earmarks the form of account we give, the way we look at things" (122). He says "A philosophical problem has the form: 'I don't know my way about'" (123).

The *Investigations* is a book of remarks, not claims, not theses, but remarks about philosophical problems. These remarks are all calculated to get one to look at the problems in question in different ways. In a literal sense of the word, Wittgenstein was concerned with appreciating, i.e., sizing up, and so dissolving philosophical difficulties. But this means that if one is to explicate particular remarks, the sensible thing to do is to explicate them in the light of the particular problems to which they are addressed.

8. Mr. Garver wants to know what Wittgenstein meant by 'criterion.' Well, what's the problem? He meant by 'criterion' something like test, or standard, or way of telling. That is, he meant what any speaker of his dialect would mean if he were using the word in familiar ways. I am inclined to suppose that most likely his use of the word 'criterion' would fit his description of the use of the word 'game,' that is, one might be able to discern a family of cases.

9. Finally, let me mention one case where Mr. Garver's theorizing clearly leads him astray.

Mr. Garver suggests that Albritton is much confused in even raising the question whether there is an inner criterion for a toothache. And he claims that the fact that Albritton even raises the question shows that his reading of Wittgenstein is inaccurate. Mr. Garver has a theory about criteria and "inner criteria" are ruled out. But then what should we say of the following remark by Wittgenstein: ". . . let us ask ourselves when we should say that *the* method that I intend comes before his mind. Now clearly we accept two different kinds of criteria for this: on the one hand the picture (of whatever kind) that at some time or other comes before his mind; on the other, the application which—in the course of time—he makes of what he imagines" (141). Evidently Wittgenstein is not a Wittgensteinian.

Am I saying that Wittgenstein's thesis is that, after all, there are inner criteria? Of course not. But neither is it his thesis that all criteria are outer criteria. He advances no theses. He is saying "Look at it this way, and now that!"

Wittgenstein concluded one set of lecture notes by saying "The seed I am most likely to sow is a certain jargon." Messrs. Shoemaker, Albritton, Malcolm, and Garver are proving him right. But that I suppose is the fate of a genius.

REJOINDERS

NEWTON GARVER

The commentators give an impressive warning that my essay cannot be regarded as either definitive or comprehensive, and they also indicate the points at which further discussion or more careful exposition is required. For these two services one must be grateful. For the most part, however, I remain unrepentant.

To Mr. Ginet's most prominent question the answer is: No, I would not deny that there are "logically necessary and sufficient conditions," because I do not know what it is I might be supposed to be denying. I do indeed think of the conditions for phenomena —i.e., for things occurring—as empirical. How could something's occurring be "conditional" upon a matter of logic? But even if a sense can be given to the phrase 'logically necessary and sufficient condition,' it would not be useful in this context: either the conception of logic involved would be Wittgenstein's, in which case it would be circular to use the phrase in explaining Wittgenstein's logical theory; or it would not, in which case its use would distort Wittgenstein's view. For the proper conception of logic is surely a large part of what is at issue.

I also reject Mr. Ginet's contention that the fluctuation between criteria and symptoms is all one-way; nor do I appreciate why he regards my two criticisms of Malcolm as incompatible. But most of his remarks are more congenial than his framing them as attacks upon me would lead one to suppose.

Mr. Siegler wonders which of the three alternative reconstructions, which he finds in my essay, is the one I intend. The answer is that I cannot acknowledge any of them as an accurate reformulation of what I said. I find his other reservations more interesting, and I regret that I have space only to say that I do not feel inclined to withdraw what I have said about Wittgenstein having a logical theory, nor about criteria being instruments, nor about the occasions when criteria are used (§§ 2–4). I also submit, anent Mr. Siegler's rather gloomy conclusion, that he is mistaken about the sort of knowledge I should have if I knew all the ways Wittgenstein uses the word 'criterion.'

Mr. Ziff's comments are the most valuable, because they are the most uncompromising and they raise several issues worthy of long and careful discussion. He is generally right where he says my remarks are unclear, and he may be right where he directly takes issue with me. But his case is not wholly convincing. A large factor is that the remarks he quotes from Wittgenstein (*Inv.* I. 288, 109, 128, 141) will not by themselves bear the weight he puts upon them. For example, it is Mr. Ziff who denies that Wittgenstein has a logical theory, not Wittgenstein himself. Wittgenstein claims not to "advance *theses* in philosophy" (*Inv.* I. 128). But do what Wittgenstein and I call "grammatical propositions" advance what he calls "theses"? And even if the logical theory I have attributed to Wittgenstein consists of "theses" about the propriety of arguments and discourse, does this entail that such theses are "philosophical"? The matter is subtle, but I should answer both questions in the negative. As Mr. Ziff insists, we cannot discount what Wittgenstein says; but what he says still needs to be interpreted, and the interpretation is not so clear-cut as Mr. Ziff supposes.

I agree that Wittgenstein was a genius. Geniuses force us to look at things in new ways, and where they have to do with ideas this characteristically involves new ways of speaking. Wittgenstein disparages himself in this regard when he refers to his contribution to our terminology as "jargon." As the potential beneficiaries, however, it would be foolish for us to join him in this disparagement.

THE PRIVATE-LANGUAGE ARGUMENT*

HECTOR-NERI CASTAÑEDA

Introduction

In the great revolution in philosophy brought about by Ludwig Wittgenstein, a prominent place is occupied by a cluster of ideas and arguments to the effect that a private language is impossible.

In sections 250-270 of his *Philosophical Investigations*, Wittgenstein does seem to be presenting *one* argument against private language in the form of a *reductio ad absurdum*. He writes:

> Let us imagine the following case. I want to keep a diary about the recurrence of a certain sensation. To this end I associate it with the sign 'E' and write this sign in a calendar for every day on which I have the sensation .... (*Inv.* I. 258)

He argues that the sign 'E' as described, as a symbol of a private language, has no meaning at all.

Similarly, Malcolm writes at the end of his now classic discussion of those sections:

> The argument that I have been outlining has the form of a *reductio ad absurdum*: Postulate a "private" language; then deduce that it is not a *language*. (*Disc.*, p. 537, his italics)

A. The Private-language thesis

The assumption for the reductio ad absurdum. Wittgenstein's thesis is that a private language is logically impossible. He seems to define a private language by saying: "*The individual words of this language are to refer to what can only be known to the person speaking; to his immediate sensations. So another person cannot understand the language*" (*Inv.* I. 243, my italics). He means to include not only sensations, but everything that has been called a "mental act." He presents himself as attacking

---

* *Editor's note*: In this symposium, as in the preceding one, many references are made to Ludwig Wittgenstein's *Philosophical Investigations*, Oxford, 1953 or 1958, and for simplicity most of these references are placed within the texts of the symposium papers. But whether within the texts, or in the footnotes, references to numbered sections of Part I of this work are given in the form, e.g., '*Inv.* I. 217,' or where the work need not again be named, simply 'I. 217'; and references to pages in Part II are given analogously. Wherever context permits, the specification of Part I or of Part II is omitted.

In Mr. Castañeda's references one other abbreviation occurs: '*Disc.*' referring to Norman Malcolm's discussion, "Wittgenstein's *Philosophical Investigations*," in *Philosophical Review*, LXIII, 1954, pp. 530–559.

the picture of all of them as objects, i.e., as private objects (*Inv.* I. 207, 222, 293, 304, etc.).

Both Wittgenstein (*Inv.* I. 243 just quoted) and Malcolm (*Disc.*, pp. 530 ff.) infer from their definition of private language that only the speaker can understand it.

Language. It is nowadays a commonplace (thanks especially to Wittgenstein's own teaching) to say that a language is a system or aggregate of rules, a system or aggregate of linguistic activities. Thus naming, describing, identifying, commanding, questioning, etc., all support one another, in different degrees and ranges, to be sure; but, e.g., *there is no naming in isolation from the rest of a language*, existing as it were in a linguistic vacuum. As Wittgenstein so beautifully puts it: ". . . a great deal of stagesetting in the language is presupposed if the mere act of naming is to make sense. And when we speak of someone's having given a name to pain, what is presupposed is the existence of the grammar of the word 'pain,' which shows the post where the new word is stationed" (*Inv.* I. 257).

Consequently, the assumption for the private-language argument cannot be that a man is trying to keep a diary with *only* the sign 'E.' We must assume that he has at his disposal a set of signs interrelated by means of a network of merely linguistic rules and a good deal more, since what Wittgenstein calls "grammar" includes a lot more than the mere tautologies of a language.

It is not clear that Wittgenstein's is the issue between a public and an *absolutely* private language. Very naturally, one would expect to find many cases of private language all linked up by a series of family resemblances, ranging off from a language *all* of whose individual words refer only to private objects. It is also worth noting that the issue private *v.* public language, as raised, has nothing to do with the extremely difficult problem concerning the *origin* of language. Even if it is a psycho-sociological law that language can be developed by groups only, that law is irrelevant to the present issue. For as Malcolm with characteristic penetration says: "It is logically possible that someone should have been born with a knowledge of the use of an expression or that it should have been produced in him by a drug" (*Disc.*, p. 544).

Private objects. Wittgenstein's definition makes the privacy of the language depend *solely* on the privacy of the objects the language is used to think about. From that definition, however, it does not follow that, e.g., a private language cannot have a single word in common with a public language. Yet, Wittgenstein himself argues:

What reason have we for calling 'E' the sign of a sensation? For *'sensation' is a word of our common language*, not one intelligible to me alone. . . . And it would not help either to say that . . . when he writes 'E,' he has something. . . . '*Has*' and '*something*' *also belong to our common language.* (*Inv.* I. 261, his italics in 'sensation' and 'something' only)

And Malcolm challenges:

> If I recognize that my mental image is the "same" as one that I had previously, how am I to know that *this public word* '*same*' describes what I recognize? (*Disc.*, p. 537, my italics)

If Wittgenstein's definition of a private language in *Inv.* I. 243 is taken as an honest effort at giving the idea of a private language a full run, it must not be understood to deny a private language all logical terms: (a) connectives, (b) inferential terms, (c) copulas, (d) quantifiers, (e) numerals, etc. Since the meanings of all these expressions have nothing to do with whether the objects talked about are private or public, it is not at all clear why a language about private objects should by that reason alone be prevented from including any of them.

Similarly, to consider a private language as having no propositions in common with any other language is also to deny it all logical signs. If a language has logical terms, then tautological propositions are bound to appear, and many of them will be translatable into other languages. Thus, a private language is one which has *some* words descriptive of private objects.

Now, there are several senses of 'private object':

(1) one which the speaker alone can (i.e., logically can) have experience of, or be acquainted with;
(2) object whose existence is (logically) determinable by the speaker alone:
  (2a) nobody else but the speaker can think (or say) with original certainty that the object exists;
  (2b) it is logically necessary that if the object exists, the speaker knows that it exists (others may know of the existence of the object, but their knowledge is not a logical consequence of the object's existence);
  (2c) the object's existence is entailed by the speaker's belief that it exists (others' belief that the object exists may be never mistaken, but it does not entail the objects' existence);
(3) objects whose possession of some characteristic A is (logically) determinable by the speaker alone:
  (3a) nobody else but the speaker can think (or say) with original certainty that the object is A;
  (3b) it is logically necessary for the speaker, and only for him, that if the object is A, he knows that it is A;

(3c) the object's being A is entailed by the speaker's, and only by the speaker's, belief that it is A;
(4) objects about which the speaker alone can determine for any first-order statement whether it is true or false of them;
(5) objects about which the speaker alone can make first-order statements, i.e., objects which only first-order predicates which the speaker alone can use, apply to;
(6) objects about which the speaker alone can make any statement at all.

In each alternative, 'can' is a logical 'can.'

The difference between (5) and (6) is that the former does, whereas the latter does not, allow other persons to refer to my private objects indirectly or vicariously, *via* my statements about them. (6) is a very extreme, empty conception of a private object, not worth discussing.

(1)–(4) do not require fully private predicates; for them it suffices that the predicates in question have only private applications, e.g., after-images and physical surfaces can have the same (or very similar) characteristics of color and shape. Thus, (1)–(4) can hold in purely private as well as in mixed languages.

What did Wittgenstein have in mind when he attacked private language in order to explode the idea of a private object? Wittgenstein attacks the fundamental idea of a private object ("if we construe the grammar of the expression of sensation on the model of 'object and name' the object drops out of consideration as irrelevant," *Inv.* I. 293; *v.* also *Inv.* I. 304; II. 207, 222, etc.). Thus it is fair to see him as attacking all types of language which involve the idea of a private object in any of the senses (1) to (4):

Or is it like this: the word 'red' means something known to everyone; and in addition, for each person, it means something known only to him? (Or perhaps rather: it *refers* to something known only to him.) (*Inv.* I. 273)

Final statement of the assumption for the reductio. We are then to assume that a certain person (to be called *Augustine Privatus*) speaks and writes a language (hereafter called *Privatish*) which is private. *Privatish contains several logical signs, which we shall assume to be identical with those of ordinary English.* In some cases we shall assume that Privatish includes *a public sub-language* of the relevant kind, whose purely public words will be supposed to be identical with their English counterparts.

B. Some Counter-Examples

Privately experienceable objects. If Wittgenstein conceived of private objects in sense (1), his thesis seems to admit of an obvious counter-example. Many philosophers and non-philosophers alike have held that one cannot (logically cannot) be acquainted with, or have experience of, someone else's sensations or after-images. These are all regarded as private in sense (1).

Privately ascertainable objects: pains. If Wittgenstein and his followers have senses (2) and (3) of 'private object' in mind, then the private-language thesis is amenable to refutation by existing counter-examples. Ordinary pains and after-images are private in those senses.

The ordinary language of pains which I employ is such that the following propositions are all logically true (or true *ex vi terminorum*):

Meaning Postulates of Pain:

A. (*Postulate of Subjectivity.*) If X has a pain Y at time t and is not distracted from it, he feels Y at t.
B. (*Postulate of Subjective Ownership.*) If X feels a pain Y at t, X has Y at t.
C. (*Postulate of Direct Access.*) If X feels a pain Y at t, and at t he is capable of thinking that he has a pain at t, and is attending to his feelings (or his mental goings-on), then at t X knows that he has Y.
D. (*Postulate of Incorrigibility.*) If X thinks attentively at t that he has a pain Y at t, then X feels Y at t.
E. (*Postulate of Subjective Thought.*) X thinks at t that he has a pain Y if and only if at t he thinks that he feels Y.
F. (*Postulate of Corrigible Access to Others.*) It is logically possible that everybody else thinks attentively at t that X has (had or will have) a pain Y at t_1 without X having Y at t_1.
G. (*Postulate of Indirect Access to Others.*) It is logically possible that X has a pain Y at t without anybody else knowing at any time that X has Y at t.

The following propositions can be derived from the postulates:

J*. (*Theorem of Limited Private Access.*) There are some kinds (or predicates) ø such that if X has a pain Y of kind ø at t, nobody else knows that X has Y at t.
J^a. (*Theorem of Qualified Private Access.*) If X has a pain Y at t, nobody else knows, whatever the time, that X has Y at t, *in the same way* that X knows that he has Y at t.

Proposition J* makes of the ordinary language of pains (as I understand it) a private language. According to it, the speaker alone can determine whether a pain of kind ø exists or not and, of course, whether the pain (in case it exists) is ø or not. Thus, pains are private in senses (2a) and (3a).

Postulates C (of Direct Access to One's Own Pains) and G (of Indirect Access to Others' Pains) entail that ordinary pains are private in sense (2b). One knows, according to them, of his own pains by merely having them. That is, one knows of them privately. Likewise, postulates D (of Incorrigibility Concerning One's Own Pains) and F (of Corrigibility Concerning Others' Pains) entail that pains are private objects in sense (2c). Therefore, the ordinary language of pains is a counter-example to Wittgenstein's thesis, if interpreted as the claim that a language employed to think about private objects is of type (2).

Finally, the same postulates C and G, or D and F entail that the speaker is, of logical necessity, in a privileged position to determine whether or not a certain predicate applies to a pain he feels. Pains are, then, private objects in both senses (3b) and (3c).

Wittgensteinians hold the view, W, that 'I know that I am in pain' is either senseless or a verbose synonym of 'I am in pain.' W suggests a reply to my claim that pains are private objects in senses (2) and (3). A Wittgensteinian may say that since it is senseless to say 'I know that I am in pain' it is senseless to say that one's own pains are objects which one alone can *know* in either sense (2) or (3); hence, it is senseless to say that one's language about one's own pains is private. Wittgensteinians have offered four arguments in support of W.

(a) The first argument runs: If a proposition is contingent, it is logically possible to believe falsely that it is true. If 'I am in pain' expressed the contingent proposition we normally take it to express, one could believe that one is in pain without being in pain. This is impossible, hence there is no such proposition that one can believe or know.

This is a howler. From 'It is impossible to believe falsely that one is in pain' it follows that it is necessary that if one believes oneself to be in pain, one's belief is true. Since 'I am in pain' cannot but be contingent, the major premise of the argument is false.

Probably Wittgensteinians mean to argue: A contingent proposition can be believed falsely to be true; if 'I am in pain' expressed a contingent proposition as we normally take it to do, the sentence 'I believed falsely at time t that I was in pain at t' would be meaningful. It is not, hence there is no such proposition.

But obviously 'I believed falsely at t that I was in pain at t' is meaningful; it expresses a conceptual contradiction; its negation is a necessary truth. In any case, the conclusion of the argument is false. 'I am in pain' uttered by me makes the same statement as 'Castañeda is in pain' uttered by you, which expresses (or is) a proposition. Furthermore, 'I am in pain' expresses something which is true or false, which can be contradicted, that has entailments, and appears as a premise in arguments. These five features together are sufficient to make the utterances of 'I am in pain' the expressions of propositions.

(b) The second argument for W runs: It is odd and out of order in ordinary language to say that one believes or thinks that one is in pain. 'I believe that p' is used to make weak assertions that p, i.e., to suggest the possibility of a mistaken belief or a doubt. There is no room for doubt or mistaken belief about one's own pains. Hence, 'I believe that I am in pain' is senseless and so is 'I know that I am in pain.'

This argument is invalid, unless 'senseless' means 'out of order or odd.' Once again, from 'There is no room for a mistaken belief' it follows that if one believes that one is in pain one's belief is true. And this explains fully why it is odd to say merely 'I believe that I am in pain,' given that this assertion suggests the possibility of a mistake.

(c) The third argument for W: In ordinary language it is odd and out of order to ask a person who has declared that he is in pain 'How do you know?' Hence, it is senseless to say 'I know that I am in pain,' unless this just means 'I am in pain.'

This is an inconclusive argument, even if 'senseless' means 'odd or out of order.' Given the fact that one cannot be mistaken about one's pains, the senselessness of the question amounts to the pointlessness of asking a person for an answer which the person knows that one already knows. The only answer to 'How do you know?' is here: 'By having the pain' or 'By attending to my feelings.' Since both persons know that they know the meanings of 'pain,' 'know,' etc., the question is quite pointless.

Nothing in the argument shows that it is even pointless—let alone nonsensical—to speak of knowing one's own pains. In making an inventory of the ways of knowing, one lists physical objects as known by perception, pains as known by feeling, or introspection, mathematical theorems as known by deduction, etc. This also refutes the fourth argument for W, which is:

(d) It is correct to speak of knowledge only when there is a question of finding out, of checking and testing. But it is absurd to suppose that one can make tests for finding out whether one is in pain or not.

Since it is correct to speak of knowing one's own pains, the major premise is false.

In sum, it is odd, because pointless, to inform another person that one believes or thinks that one is in pain, or to insist that one knows that one is in pain. But this fact about ordinary *reporting* in no way shows that there are no facts that would not be reported if one were to make pointless assertions. The pointlessness of the assertions is not only compatible with their intelligibility, but even presupposes it. I conclude, therefore, that the ordinary language of pains is still a mixed private language in several senses and remains, therefore, a counter-example against Wittgenstein's thesis.

C. The Private-Language Argument

The charge: possibility of mistakes. From the assumption formulated above we are, according to Malcolm, to deduce that Privatish is *not* a language. Since a language is an aggregate of rules, it would suffice to show that in using Privatish, Privatus cannot be following rules.

Wittgenstein's argument is very compact, but the following unpacking seems to be true to what he had in mind. A rule is essentially the sort of thing that can be followed (obeyed or satisfied) or not, and also the sort of thing that can be misapplied; a person trying to follow a rule can make a mistake and end up by not following it. Thus, the possibility of not acting in accordance with a rule is of the essence and substance of a rule. Hence it must be possible for Privatus to make mistakes in the exercise of the rules constituting Privatish. If there is no way in which Privatus can misapply the signs belonging to Privatish, then this is not made up of rules and is, therefore, not a language. Naturally, Wittgenstein does claim that it is impossible for Privatus to make mistakes in using the (so-called) signs belonging to Privatish. This claim has been rounded out by Malcolm as follows:

1. Now how is it to be decided whether I have used the word consistently [i.e., correctly]?
2. What will be the difference between my having used it consistently and its *seeming* to me that I have?
3. Or has this distinction vanished?
4. "Whatever is going to seem right to me is right." (*Inv.* I. 258).
5. "And that only means that here we can't talk about 'right'." (*Ibid.*)
6. If the distinction between 'correct' and 'seems correct' has disappeared, then so has the concept *correct*.
7. It follows that the "rules" of my private language are only *impressions* of rules (*Inv.* I. 259).
8. My impression that I follow a rule does not confirm that I follow a rule, unless there can be something that will prove my impression correct.
9. And the something cannot be another impression—for:
10. This would be "as if someone were to buy several copies of the morning paper to assure himself that what it said was true" (*Inv.* I. 165).
11. The proof that I am following a rule must appeal to something *independent* of my impression that I am.
12. If in the nature of the case there cannot be such an appeal, then my private language does not have *rules*.

These are Malcolm's sentences and quotations, in sequence (*Disc.*, p. 532), but the numbering is mine.

The first remark to be made is that Wittgenstein's and Malcolm's discussions relate to the assumption that Privatus wrote the isolated symbol 'E' on a calendar, while he is not given the privilege of using the rest of Privatish. As we said this is an unfair *reductio ad absurdum*.

The second remark is that the quotation from Malcolm does *not* prove that in a private language the distinction between 'correct' and 'seems correct' is missing—except in as much as this follows from sentences 8 and 9 or 11 and 12. The first three sentences are questions, *not* reasons, which simply formulate the issue in slightly different ways. Sentence 4 formulates, precisely, the *conclusion* to be established ("Whatever is going to seem right to me [or Privatus] is right"). Sentence 5 is a consequence of the fourth one—but it cannot be asserted unless the fourth is established. The next assertion, in sentence 6, follows from the preceding one, and so depends on the thesis formulated in the sentence 4, which *still* is to be proven. Sentence 7, I think, is a logical truth ("It follows that . . ."), *viz.*, that something follows from sentence 6; but what comes after the word 'follows' is still hanging in mid-air, and will be there, until what the fourth sentence asserts is shown to be true. The next two assertions, in sentences 8 and 9 can be taken to constitute the premises of an argument. The tenth sentence gives, as a reason for the ninth, an analogy, which by itself proves nothing. Sentences 11 and 12 look like a repetition of sentences 8 and 9. But there is a difference.

Thus, to examine Malcolm's and Wittgenstein's argument in their *reductio ad absurdum*, we must first focus our logical microscopes on 8 and 9:

8. My impression that I follow a rule does not confirm that I follow a rule, unless there can be something that will prove my impression correct.
9. And the something cannot be another impression.

Clearly, these two assertions by themselves do not entail that a private rule, or a private language, is impossible. To prove this we need a minor premise.

9A. The user of a private language can avail himself of impressions only.

Unfortunately, 9A is far from being obviously true. It might be thought that all private objects are impressions. But even if this were to be granted, 9A would still be true only of the purely private languages. With the equation of private object and impression, propositions 8 and 9 would then amount to the statement that the user of a purely private language cannot resort to his private objects to check whether he is following a rule of his language.

But neither this proposition nor the equation of impression and private object is self-evident. It is not even clear how one should attempt to prove them. At any rate, the argument so produced would not exclude the possibility of a mixed language.

Let us turn now to the alternative premises:

11. The proof that I am following a rule must appeal to something *independent* of my impression that I am.
12. If in the nature of the case there cannot be such an appeal, then my private language does not have *rules*.

Sentence 12 seems to be saying essentially the same as 8, but the meaning of 12 is clarified by 11, which differs from 9, which supplements the meaning of 8. Sentences 11–12 do not forbid Privatus to check whether he is following a rule of Privatish by means of other impressions of his; they only require that he make use of impressions which are independent of his impression that he is following the rule (correctly). They do not beg the question against a purely private language. In short, 11 and 12 are very reasonable; the only restriction one should impose on them is *that they must also hold for public languages*.

No doubt, from 11 and 12 it does follow that Privatish is not a language—provided that we can establish the antecedent of 12:

12A. In the nature of the case there cannot be an appeal to something independent of Privatus' impression that he is using a rule of Privatish correctly, to check whether his use is in fact correct or not.

But this proposition must be established. Indeed, given the direction of the argument, it is precisely the substance of Wittgenstein's thesis.

The charge reformulated: self-correction. Can Privatus avail himself of something independent of his impression that he is following a rule of Privatish to check whether he is in fact following it? If there is something which meets the requirements, then the argument of Wittgenstein and Malcolm cannot succeed, unless it follows some line different from the one now being discussed.

Before proceeding any further, it should be noticed that the above formulation of the issue is misleading and biased. It presents Privatus as deciding whether a certain utterance of his accords with a certain rule. The contention is that the utterance is arbitrarily chosen so that it is legitimate to generalize to all utterances in Privatish. But the initial setup is distorted. We cannot require Privatus to know the formulation of the rule in question.

There is an insight in saying that language is a set of rules; but it is misleading to say that to use language is to *obey* or *follow* rules.

For the most part one's actions exhibit certain regularities, which one would describe as actions in accordance with certain rules. But one is not obeying or trying to follow a rule. If an action is successful, i.e., if there are no unexpected obstacles, there is no question about having followed a rule correctly. Inasmuch as it makes sense to say that when a person speaks or writes he applies the rules governing the use of the expressions he employs, *linguistic rules have to be precisely rules which are much more often than not applied correctly without their correct application being an issue at all*, as Wittgenstein well knew (cf. *Inv.* I. 207). If every sound or word were uttered from the conception of its rule, we would have to be aware of the rules in question in a language or in words (including the logical words), altogether different from the language or words we are to use in following those rules. But we would need another language to formulate and try to obey those rules, if every use of language is a case of obeying rules, and so on *ad infinitum*. This is a platitude, but it is worth emphasizing, for it would be bad logic to suppose that Privatus must decide for each rule he abides by in making a Privatish utterance, that he is following it. He should be supposed, like any speaker of a public language, both:

(a) to be using Privatish words (correctly or incorrectly) without having to *think*, let alone decide, that each one is used correctly, and
(b) to be using most of them correctly as a matter of course.

As Wittgenstein has greatly emphasized, a language (and, naturally, he is speaking of a public language) has to have "enough regularity" (*Inv.* I. 207), i.e., people cannot always be mistaken in their use of words; for the most part they must get to use them rightly (see also *Inv.* I. 222–224, 245). Indeed, as he goes on to stress: "If language is to be a means of communication there must be agreement not only in definitions but also (queer as this may sound) in judgments . . . what we call 'measuring' is partly determined by a certain constancy in results of measurement" (*Inv.* I. 242).

Thus, in the case of Privatus and Privatish it is fair to assume, insofar as for the purpose of our *reductio ad absurdum* we are assuming that Privatish is a language, that Privatus is for the most part consistent in his use of Privatish, that his use of signs possesses "enough regularity," and also that he holds certain true beliefs about his private objects, which beliefs are the counterparts of the judgments agreed on in the case of a public language.

Wittgenstein or Malcolm cannot imply that Privatus must decide whether each word is used correctly or not. All that they may argue is: (i) that it must be *possible* for Privatus to misapply the rules of Privatish, (ii) that it must be *possible* for Privatus to know that he has made a mistake, and (iii) that he must know how to correct his mistakes.

Examination of the charge. Now Privatish is not a language, if Wittgenstein's and Malcolm's contention is true that Privatus cannot appeal to something independent of his impression that he is following a rule to check whether he is in fact following it or not. But is this contention true?

It is false. Privatus can resort to practically all the "things" to which the speakers of public, or of ordinary, languages have recourse —he can do this even in the case in which Privatish is a *purely* private language. In general, to determine whether or not a word has been correctly used, we resort to the objects of our experience, the noises or marks which constitute our language, the memories of past utterances, the entailments among our concepts, and the generalizations which relate different kinds of objects. In the case of a public language, we can ask a fellow speaker, or we can receive his unsolicited corrections. This is, of course, not open to Privatus. Yet that circumstance cannot be at this juncture an objection against Privatish being a language. The very issue is, in part, whether that circumstance *is* a necessary condition for a language.

One thing, however, is definitely clear, namely, *that a person possesses a language only inasmuch as he is capable of self-correction.* A person has not learned color words or English, unless he is able to use his symbols independently of another's approval; but then he will know how to correct his occasional mistakes.

Privatus *qua* speaker of Privatish has his experiences and the objects, private or public, which he apprehends in them, his memories of previous utterances, the words of Privatish, the logical connections among these, and the generalizations which link some objects to others. Clearly, most of them are independent of his impression that he is using a certain word correctly. Even his memory images that on, say, five occasions in the past he described a private object as A may be wholly independent of his present impression that 'A' applies to the same or some similar object.

Privatus can correct his mistaken uses of words in essentially the same way in which we normally correct our linguistic errors. For instance, an English speaker can correct his misapplication of a word simply by noting that the object is not what he called it; he may say: "That red, . . . I mean, brown chair. . . ." Here we have a linguistic self-correction. If a rule of language was not followed (I suppose, the one governing the use of the expression 'red' or 'brown') and a correction was made, then Privatus may be correcting his having not followed a linguistic rule of Privatish in a case in which he says: "This A, that is, this B . . . ," where 'A' and 'B' may very well be private predicates. Often, in the English example, the speaker knows of his slip on hearing his utterance of the word 'red,' and clearly, both his hearing of it and the noise he hears are independent of his impression that he was using the correct word. Exactly the same can be said of Privatus and his Privatish expressions 'A' and 'B.' The possibility of such a case provides a counter-example to Wittgenstein's and Malcolm's contention.

It may be argued that the English speaker can correct himself without having anything at all independent of his impression that he used the word 'red' correctly, that he can correct his slip without hearing his words, etc. Then it is argued that in the case of an ordinary language, which is assumed to be public throughout, since private languages are claimed to be impossible, a person can correct himself without the aid of anything independent of his impression that he has used a word correctly. *But then it is bad logic to require a private language to meet a condition which is not regarded as necessary for language.* It may be replied that in the English case, others can in principle correct the speakers. This is certainly true. But it cannot be adduced as a reason by itself, for the argument is precisely intended to prove that *because* of the fact that others cannot correct him Privatus cannot correct himself. The fact in question has been assumed from the very beginning; the issue is the *because*.

To belabor the point let us consider another situation. A person can become aware of, and correct, a slip thanks to his wanting to make a certain inference and finding himself using the right generalization. For instance, one may say "This is an elephant; since every rhinoceros has a horn on its nose, this, I mean, this rhinoceros, not this elephant, will have a horn on its nose." Here the items independent of the impression attached to the first use of the word 'elephant' that it is a correct use are (or may very well be): the desire to make the valid reasoning in question (which requires the premise "This is a rhinoceros"), the awareness of uttering or thinking that every rhinoceros has a horn on its nose, the utterance, the uttered premise "This is an elephant" (whose lingering presence to the mind is necessary as part of the inference), the awareness (or "feeling" or impression) that the validity of the inference requires the two premises to have a common term at those places, etc. These are not all impressions (in any normal sense of the word), but even if impressions, they are independent of the impression that the word 'elephant' was used correctly. There is nothing in the case which requires that other persons can correct the speaker, even if merely in principle. Privatus may do exactly the same while using Privatish.

Furthermore, on the assumption, as presented in the final statement of the assumption for the *reductio*, that Privatish is a private language, Privatus is automatically allowed to avail himself of other items which are independent of his impression that he has used a certain term correctly. He may write one afternoon, under our telescopes:

(a) This is an E. Since all A's are followed by B's, this A will be followed by a B.
There is a B.

Suppose, in accordance with the assumption *to be shown* to be self-contradictory, that 'A,' 'E' and 'B' are purely private predicates. Clearly, Privatus can a few minutes later (as measured by our clocks) read the entry (a) in his diary. He reads it aloud, stops at the symbol 'A,' scratches it off and writes just above it the symbol 'E.' Here, in addition to the items mentioned above, he has the written text and his visual perceptions, which are certainly independent of his impression that he used the word 'A' correctly.

I conclude, then, that if for the purpose of a *reductio ad absurdum* it is fully assumed that Privatus possesses a private language, i.e., a whole system of symbols whose use is interrelated, habits of using such symbols, and enough private objects which manifest sufficient regularities, then Privatus has everything necessary for linguistic self-correction, which after all is really the necessary condition at issue for the possession of a language. The symbols of the language, the private objects themselves, the logical or grammatical interrelations among the former, the empirical generalizations linking the latter, the memories of previous uses of language, are all available to the speaker of a private language. Hence, the important premises 9A and 12A quoted above (under *The charge: possibility of mistakes*), necessary for the success of the Wittgenstein-Malcolm argument under discussion, cannot be established.

First rejoinder: infinity of doubts. It is sometimes argued that the speaker of a private language can never be sure that he is using a (private) sign correctly, even if he has something to test his use of the sign for correctness. Suppose Privatus has something, say B, against which he can test his present use of the sign 'A'; surely, he can misinterpret B; so he can be in doubt as to whether he is using B correctly; thus he would have to appeal to something else, say C, to test the correctness of his application of B; but again, he can misinterpret or misapply C, and so on *ad infinitum*.

The argument is a telling one. It shows that there can be no *logical* certainty that a descriptive word has been used consistently throughout. But this is also true of public languages. If I say "This is red," and you tell me that it is blue, to be sure that my use of 'red' is incorrect I must be sure that your use of 'blue' is correct. But to be sure of that I must be sure that it is true that you have in fact said "No, it is blue," and for this I must be sure that you are there, are not deaf-mute, were talking to me, etc. And each of these *can* also be subjected to a doubt. So, if to be certain that a word has been used correctly (or incorrectly) I must reach a point where no doubt is possible, then public languages also fall under the axe of the present argument. This is a *reductio ad absurdum* of the rejoinder.

Second rejoinder: "*Mistakes, not slips.*" Often a defender of Wittgenstein's thesis argues that the issue whether or not Privatus can misapply the rules of Privatish and correct himself has not been touched by such discussion. He might insist that a relevant mistake and a relevant correction are a mistaken belief of Privatus and his correction of such a belief about his private objects or about the rules of Privatish. The Wittgensteinian would argue that whatever Privatus believes to be A will have to be A, for it is so for him and he has nothing independent against which to check his *belief*.

A verbal slip is as good as any other case of not doing what the rule prescribes. The essential feature of rules, which distinguishes them from descriptions of action, is that they can hold (be true or valid) regardless of what the agent (for whom they prescribe some action) performs, while at the same time they differ from grammatical or analytic statements in that they can be fulfilled (satisfied) or not. Whether it is because of a slip or a misinterpretation or something else that an agent does not satisfy the rule is completely immaterial.

Is it not true that if Privatus follows the rules of Privatish, he calls every case of A 'A'? Then, since in the case of a slip he calls an instance of A 'E' and not 'A,' he did not follow, or write in accordance with, all the rules of the Privatish language.

Let us accept then that the possibility of verbal slips is not enough to show that Privatish conceived as having objects of type (6) or type (5)—as we listed them at the outset—is a language; let us take it as established that Privatish must allow Privatus the possibility of holding some false belief. As in the case of mistakes in doing something in accordance with a rule, we must concede: (i) that Privatus must be in a position to have some false beliefs, even if in fact he never does; (ii) that Privatus must be in principle capable of knowing of some of his false beliefs that they are false; and (iii) that Privatus must be able to correct some of his mistakes in belief.

It is quite apparent that Privatus can make predictions about his private objects, and those predictions can turn out to be false. Hence, Privatish does not prevent Privatus from entertaining false beliefs.

Suppose that Privatus calls an object a 'B' if it is M and becomes P while remaining M. Then he can be mistaken and find out that he is mistaken when he says that a certain object is a B on the evidence that it is M. However, it may be replied that Privatus cannot be mistaken about something being M, provided that he is using the term 'M' correctly.

Suppose that Privatus cannot have a false belief about his present directly experienceable private objects or pains, unless he has forgotten the meaning of the relevant terms. But even this is not so simple as it looks. The application of every predicate involves an implicit comparison with both previous and later applications, as well as an implicit connection between the predicate in question and other predicates. Thus, one can be mistaken about those implicit features which constitute the grammar of the predicate. Privatus can have a doubt as to whether something he is experiencing is an M or not only because he has forgotten the meaning of 'M,' without this entailing the absurdity that he lacks even the faintest idea of what an M is like while he can formulate his doubt about the object being M or not. Forgetting the meaning of 'M' is not a black-or-white situation. One may have forgotten the meaning of 'orange' *enough* so as not to be able to tell whether a given object is orange or not; but one can have the doubt because one knows that orange is a color and knows that it keeps certain similarities to red, for instance. One can even resolve one's doubt by testing for the appearance of the color of the object in question by mixing red and yellow pigments, if one remembers that orange is thus producible. And this need not involve the claim that orange is defined as the color obtained by mixing red and yellow pigments. All that one needs is to hold fast to the generalization that orange is as a matter of empirical fact so produced. It is an essential part of the meaning of a word that it must enter into well-grounded generalizations. Likewise, one may even decide whether a certain sensation is of pain or not by cutting oneself and experiencing a typical case of pain. Again, here it is only necessary that the empirical link between pains and wounds of the relevant sort be well established.

Once again, we find that if Privatus is allowed to support a given application of an expression of Privatish with the rest of the Privatish language, he can avail himself of the objects of his experience, the other expressions, the entailment relationships, and the empirical generalizations, and thus he can check whether *some* of his beliefs are true or false.

The rejoinder, then, is met. Privatish allows Privatus to have some false beliefs, to experience some doubts about certain facts (or propositions) formulable in the purely private part of Privatish, and to resolve some of those doubts.

Further rejoinder: other persons' corrections. We have encountered the suggestion that other persons' corrections are (in principle) necessary for the acquisition of the concept of *correct*. At some place Malcolm, for instance, alleges that "on the private-language hypothesis, no one can teach me what the correct use of 'same' is" (*Disc.*, p. 536). Wittgenstein expresses himself in the same vein:

"Before I judge that two images which I have are the the same, I must recognize them as the same." And when that has happened, how am I to know that the word 'same' describes what I recognize? Only if I can express my recognition in some other way, and *if it is possible for someone else to teach me that 'same' is the correct word here.* (*Inv.* I. 378, my italics)

Here the argument is not that Privatus *has* not learned from others the correct use of a word, but that he *could* not have learned it from others.

It is true that in the case of a purely private language nobody else can teach the speaker how to use a private predicate. This is a trivial consequence of the definition of private language. But the major premise of the argument is not obvious at all: that if nobody else can teach Privatus the use of some word he does not know how to use it. Indeed, the argument along the present lines just reduces to the proof of that conditional. We have a right to expect an argument to show that if other persons' corrections are not available the whole idea of *correct* is not available, either.

The need for others' corrections. Even though neither Malcolm nor Wittgenstein has proved that Privatus' concept of correct use must come from outside Privatish, may this not be so? Our discussion (in *The charge reformulated: self-correction,* and later) seems already to show that it need not be so. Nevertheless, somebody may stress that if it is *logically* impossible for another person to correct Privatus' use of language, then he cannot tell whether his use is correct or not. But 'Nobody else can correct Privatus' does *not* entail 'Privatus cannot correct himself,' regardless of whether 'can' expresses here a logical modality or not.

It seems strange that a *mere* logical possibility of being corrected by somebody else could serve as an antidote against Privatus' mistakes. To know that he has made a mistake and to know how to correct it require a good deal more than the purely abstract possibility that if somebody were to speak Privatus' language such a person could tell him what he did wrong and why. If nobody is *in fact* around to correct Privatus' mistakes, or if nobody can correct his mistakes simply because nobody around him speaks his public language, then he will be in just as bad a predicament as if his language were private (in the sense characterized in *Inv.* I. 243). He would be left entirely to himself and his mistakes, without any help which could in fact enable him to distinguish the correct from the incorrect. As I see it, if it were legitimate to require seriously the possibility of other persons' corrections, it would be impossible to have the case of a single person speaking a public language, e.g., Dalmatian or ordinary English. Yet at the end of the nineteenth century there was just Antonio Udina who spoke Dalmatian, and it makes sense to suppose that World War III may leave on earth exactly one English speaker with no knowledge of any other language. Obviously, whatever the last speaker of English were to say would be right—insofar as nobody else could correct him. It would be of no avail to say "Well, if there were another English speaker near him, such a speaker *could* correct him." The issue is not whether he *could* have a language, but whether he *has* one. The point is that he would in fact be uttering sounds under no checks whatever—except what he remembered and what he experienced.

Indeed, it is not even clear that a person who spends some time in isolation would be actually using rules—if we are to require that other persons' checks be necessary. Clearly, the longer he remains alone the greater are his chances of making mistakes, and, once again, the *mere* abstract logical possibility of another person's corrections is too tenuous to be of real help. It is very difficult to see how the mere fact that *if* another person were beside the isolated speaker he could correct him, provides that speaker with checks and criteria and the conception of *correct* and the conception of *true*, even though *in fact* there is nobody beside him and he hears no voices approving of his use of language or confirming his beliefs! The only positive way in which the isolated speaker can detect and correct his mistakes is by actually checking his assertions or beliefs against the objects as they appear to him or as he remembers them—exactly as Privatus has been doing all along while using Privatish.

It may be adduced that there is a difference between Privatus on the one hand, and on the other Antonio Udina (when he became the last speaker of Dalmatian), Robinson Crusoe, and an isolated speaker of, say, Spanish. These persons have all *acquired the concept* of correctness from their elders, whereas Privatus did not; and it may be alleged that the issue is not whether a person's uses of words are corrected or not, but whether the person has come into possession of the concept of correctness. Thus, according to this allegation, Antonio Udina's knowledge of Dalmatian may deteriorate if nobody can in practice correct him, but since he has acquired the concept of correct use he can go on speaking Dalmatian indefinitely. This is an exciting line of argument, but it is irrelevant to the private language issue. As noticed at the beginning, the mode of acquisition of the use of words, i.e., of a concept, is not a characteristic feature of language: "It is logically possible that someone [why not either Privatus or Antonio Udina indifferently?] should have been born with a knowledge of the use of an expression or that it should have been produced in him by a drug" (*Disc.*, p. 544).

COMMENTS

V. C. CHAPPELL

Castañeda's paper contains a good deal that I cannot accept, and my general judgment is that though he makes a number of valuable points in his examination of what he calls "the private-language argument" his case against Wittgenstein and Malcolm is, as a whole, unsuccessful.

I shall comment on two things specifically: (A) what Castañeda calls "the assumption for the private language argument," or in other words what he claims the expression 'private language' means for Wittgenstein and Malcolm and hence what he claims is the view that Wittgenstein and Malcolm, in their arguments against a private language, are attacking; and (B) Castañeda's own attack upon the private-language argument, as he understands it, which argument he ascribes to Wittgenstein although it is Malcolm's statement of it that he actually discusses. I shall claim, regarding (A), that there is no warrant for attributing Castañeda's "assumption" to Wittgenstein and Malcolm and in fact good reason for denying that they do or would accept it; and, regarding (B), that Castañeda's main counter-argument to Wittgenstein's (or anyhow Malcolm's) argument, even given his interpretation of it, is faulty.

(A) According to Castañeda, "Wittgenstein's thesis is that a private language is logically impossible" (p. 88). This thesis, he says, is supported by an argument of the *reductio ad absurdum* form, and he approves Malcolm's characterization of Wittgenstein's procedure: "postulate a 'private' language; then deduce that it is not a *language*." But what is this "private language" that is so postulated? Castañeda cites a passage from the *Investigations* in which, he says, Wittgenstein "seems to define a private language": "The individual words of this language are to refer to what can only be known to the person speaking; to his immediate private sensations. So another person cannot understand the language" (*Inv*. I. 243). But this definition, if it is that, may not be complete; as Castañeda notes, this passage does not make altogether clear what the "language" in question is. So this remains to be determined. Wittgenstein himself is of little help here, though he does refer again to the "language" of 243 in later passages. In *Inv*. I. 256, e.g., he considers "the language which describes my inner experiences and which only I myself can understand." But he really tells us no more about this "language" in this passage; he only makes more explicit what was surely explicit enough in 243, that not being understandable by anyone other than the speaker is a necessary condition for something's being a "private language." Again, in 258 Wittgenstein presents a case which is plainly meant to be an example of the "language" referred to in 243 and 256. This is the case in which I "keep a diary about the recurrence of a certain sensation," making use of the "sign 'E.' " But here again, the only thing that is clear from the text about the "language" which my use of 'E' constitutes or perhaps belongs to is that I alone am capable of understanding it. And I think there is no other passage in the *Investigations* in which any more than this is said about the postulated "language" of 243 and following.

Perhaps then Wittgenstein intended the condition stated in these passages to be sufficient as well as necessary for something's being a "private language." This is, I think, the most plausible view to take, and I believe it is the view that Malcolm takes. The specification given *is* complete; what is said is all that is meant to be true of the postulated "language." Castañeda, however, thinks otherwise. Our assumption regarding the diary keeper of *Inv.* I. 258, he says, "cannot be that [he] is trying to keep a diary with *only* the sign 'E.' " Rather, "we must assume that he has at his disposal a set of signs interrelated by means of a network of merely linguistic rules and a good deal more" (p. 89). But why must we make this assumption? The nearest thing to an explicit answer to this question that I can find in Castañeda's text is this, that if we did not we should not be taking the "definition of a private language in *Inv.* 243 . . . as an honest effort at giving the idea of a private language a full run" (p. 90). Or as he later puts it, the *reductio ad absurdum* would, in this case, be "unfair" (p. 96). Castañeda's reasoning seems to be as follows. A private language is, after all, a language; that is what it is *called*. And a language, as Wittgenstein himself has taught us, "is a system or aggregate of rules, a system or aggregate of linguistic activities" (p. 89). Hence the postulated "private language" must be such a system or aggregate, and this means that it must not be denied "all logical terms" and must not be considered "as having no propositions in common with any other language" (p. 90).

Now this reasoning, I submit, is inconclusive at best. To "postulate" something for the purpose of reducing it to absurdity is not, or not necessarily, to suppose that it *is* what it is *referred to as*; it is not to attribute to it all of the features which things correctly called by its name do or must have. One does not confer existence or a nature upon something by "postulating" it in this way, any more than one confers existence upon something by mentioning it; we have only to recall Russell's and Quine's worries about negative existential statements to be clear about this. Thus, the barber who shaves all and only those who do not shave themselves is not a man, nor is he not a man. To argue that he must be a man is like arguing that Hamlet's grandfather must have been a Dane or that the Loch Ness Monster must have a tail. In each case the question as to what the mentioned subject is or has simply does not apply. Of course there must be some warrant for referring to a postulated entity in the way that one does, for calling it by that name rather than some other. But this may be provided if the entity be given some of the features necessary to the things that are normally and correctly called by that name; it need not be given all of them. Typically, indeed, a *reductio ad absurdum* argument proceeds as follows: a postulated entity, referred to as it is because it has some of the features necessary to the actually existing things that are (correctly) referred to in this way, is shown not to have certain further features necessary to such things because the features which it is postulated to have logically rule out its having these further features. Wittgenstein's private-language argument, as I see it, conforms to this pattern. A private language is postulated; we call it a language because it is supposed to have words, and these are supposed to be used to refer, a linguistic activity. But, so the argument runs, because the supposed referents of these supposed words are "private," in a certain special sense, reference to them is in fact impossible, and the supposed words are not words at all, from which it follows that the supposed language which they constitute or belong to is no language after all.

It is clear, I think, that Wittgenstein *is* merely "postulating" a private language in the *Investigations* passages to which Castañeda refers. In the portion of 243 immediately preceding that in which Castañeda finds his "definition" of a private language, Wittgenstein says that we are to consider whether a private language is "thinkable"—or, in Miss Anscombe's translation, whether we could *imagine* any such thing—in other words, whether any such thing is possible. There is no question here of some *existing* thing's *being* a language, or of its *not* being one. The question rather is whether any *such* thing as a private language *could* exist—and the content of the "such" here is given in the immediately following "definition."

If Wittgenstein does argue as I have suggested, then not only is the attribution to him of Castañeda's "assumption" unwarranted, it is positively implausible. For if Wittgenstein does want to show that the postulated private language cannot have certain features that any language must have, then it would certainly be odd for him to build those very features into his conception of a private language. And yet this is what he would be doing if Castañeda were right. For it is (roughly) just the absence of "logical terms" and of what, in Castañeda's view, this entails that makes the postulated private language not a language, according to Wittgenstein. Besides which, there is a passage in the *Investigations* which strongly suggests, if it does not quite state, that the diary keeper's "language" is to have no terms in common with "our common language," including, one would think, Castañeda's "logical terms." This is *Inv.* I. 261, which Castañeda quotes, oddly enough, without grasping its import for his interpretation of Wittgenstein's position.[1]

But this is not the worst of it. As far as I can see, Castañeda, by attributing his "assumption for the private-language argument" to Wittgenstein, all but begs the main question of his paper, the question of the cogency of Wittgenstein's argument. For Castañeda rests his case against the argument primarily on the premise that the postulated private language does have "logical terms," with all that he thinks this entails—which, by the time the fray is actually joined, has become a good deal: when "for the purpose of a *reductio ad absurdum* it is fully assumed that Privatus [the diary keeper] possesses a private language, [what is assumed is that he has] a whole system of symbols whose use is interrelated, habits of using such symbols, and enough private objects which manifest sufficient regularities" (p. 101). I shall argue shortly that Castañeda's case is faulty even on this premise. But that aside, his case is surely not successful if the premise in question is not Wittgenstein's. And in the absence of any convincing reason for thinking that it is, Castañeda's mere claim that it "must be" smacks strongly of a *petitio*.

There is one curious statement in Castañeda's paper which bears on this point. On page 96, after quoting the passage in which Malcolm states (what Castañeda accepts as) Wittgenstein's argument, Castañeda says that "Wittgenstein's and Malcolm's discussions relate to the assumption that Privatus wrote the isolated symbol 'E' on a calendar, while he is not given the privilege of using the rest of Privatish [i.e., the private language conceived in accordance with Castañeda's 'assumption,' which is to say as containing 'logical terms']. As we said, this is an unfair *reductio ad absurdum*." The curious thing is that Wittgenstein and Malcolm should not be trusted to determine what should and should not be allowed to Privatus—as if it were not they who introduced the notion of a private language in the first place! Castañeda here, I think, gives away the show.

---

[1] *Inv.* I. 261 begins: "What reason have we for calling 'E' the sign for a *sensation*. For 'sensation' is a word of our common language, not of one intelligible to me alone. So the use of this word stands in need of a justification which everybody understands." *Editor's note.*

In any case, I conclude that Castañeda's attribution of his "assumption for the private-language argument" to Wittgenstein and Malcolm is both unwarranted and implausible, and besides begs, or comes close to begging, the larger question of the soundness of the private-language argument, at least as Wittgenstein and Malcolm themselves understand it.

(B) If the argument that Castañeda attacks is not the argument that Wittgenstein and Malcolm have in mind, then Castañeda has no case against *them*, whether or not he begs any questions in attributing his version of the argument to them. But I want now to show that Castañeda's case is not even successful against his own version of the private-language argument, and hence that his attack on Wittgenstein and Malcolm miscarries twice over.

The crux of the argument, as Castañeda understands it, is the claim that "it is impossible for Privatus to make mistakes in using the (so-called) signs belonging to Privatish" or "in the exercise of the rules constituting Privatish" (p. 95). Castañeda grants (what he takes to be Wittgenstein's view) that "if there is no way in which Privatus can misapply the signs belonging to Privatish, then this is not made up of rules and is, therefore, not a language" (*ibid.*). Castañeda also grants that Privatus cannot misapply the sign 'E,' e.g., if it is not possible to prove that his use of 'E' on a given occasion is or is not correct, and if it is not possible for him to know that he has misapplied 'E' and correct his mistake. Wittgenstein and Malcolm argue that no proof of the correctness of any use of 'E' is possible and that the user of a private language can neither know of nor correct linguistic mistakes; the very notion of correctness is out of place here. It follows, so their argument concludes, that the user of a private language cannot make mistakes. It is this argument, specifically, that Castañeda attacks. One of its necessary premises, he says, "cannot be established" (p. 101). In fact what he claims is that the premise in question is *false*. In either case, what he should claim thence is that Malcolm's and Wittgenstein's conclusion is without warrant, but again, what he does claim is that the conclusion is false: Privatus *can* make mistakes. Castañeda does not, so far as I can tell, argue explicitly for this stronger claim, but his reasoning seems to be this: what makes the Wittgensteinian-Malcolmian premise referred to false is the (alleged) fact that Privatish is just like our ordinary language in certain respects. In particular, Privatus "can resort to practically all the 'things' to which the speakers of public, or of ordinary, languages have recourse" in order to prove the correctness of some one of his uses of 'E' and to recognize and correct any linguistic mistakes he might make. Since, then, it is possible for the speaker of ordinary language to make linguistic mistakes, so too is it possible for Privatus to do so.

It is precisely here that Castañeda seems to me to beg the question as to the soundness of Wittgenstein's and Malcolm's argument. His claim that Privatus "can resort to practically all the 'things' to which the speakers of public, or of ordinary, languages have recourse" (p. 99) seems to me to be founded directly and only on his "assumption" that the private language discussed by Wittgenstein, being a language, has "logical terms." And this assumption, as I have indicated, seems to me to have no other basis than that Castañeda's critique of Wittgenstein requires it. But it is not this point that I am trying to establish now. Rather, what I now want to show is that the "things" to which, according to Castañeda, Privatus "can resort" are such that *either* an appeal to them would not prove the correctness of anything, *or* the claim that Privatus can resort to them is inconsistent with the original and explicit stipulation regarding the use of the sign 'E,' e.g., that 'E' be used to refer to a "private" object and that it be intelligible to no one but its user. In other words, I want to show that Castañeda's case against Wittgenstein and Malcolm is faulty even if they do hold the view that he ascribes to them, of what a private language is or could be. For whether or not this language includes "logical terms," with whatever else this entails, some of its terms must be such that no one but the speaker can understand them, and this because they are used to refer to objects which only the speaker can know about. This much Wittgenstein says, explicitly; it is the presence of such "private" terms, after all, that makes Privatish a private language. Hence it is Privatus' use of *these* terms that must be subject to mistakes, correction, and proof of correctness, whatever other terms Privatish contains and whatever is true of these. My claim will be that recourse to the "things" to which Castañeda says Privatus can have recourse, in order to prove the correctness or incorrectness of some application of a term, is either fruitless or impossible when the term in question is private, and hence that, at the very least, Castañeda has not established that Privatus can make mistakes in using the private terms of Privatish.

How do Wittgenstein and Malcolm back their claim that the user of a private language cannot make linguistic mistakes, that e.g. the diary keeper of *Inv.* I. 258 cannot misapply the sign 'E'? Castañeda confines his attention to the sketch of Wittgenstein's reasoning that is given by Malcolm (*Disc.*, p. 532). According to Malcolm, to misapply a word is to violate the rule which governs its (correct) application. In the case of 'E,' the rule can only be that 'E' be used consistently, i.e., used for the same sort of thing on each occasion; since 'E' is a private word, the question of whether the speaker's use of it agrees with others' use of it cannot arise. But now a rule cannot be violated, or indeed followed, unless it is possible to prove that a given use of language does or does not conform to it—in the case of 'E,' unless it is possible to prove that the diary keeper's application of 'E' on a given occasion is consistent or inconsistent, with his previous applications. But how is this to be done by the user of a private sign? What does the diary keeper have to go on? He may be convinced that he is using 'E' in the way he has done, but his conviction, or as Malcolm says, his impression, that he is following his rule for 'E,' by itself, is insufficient. For my conviction or impression that such and such is so, counts for something only in case it is possible to distinguish my *being right* in thinking what I do, from its *seeming* to me that I am right; otherwise the very notion of "right" does not apply. In Malcolm's words, "My impression that I follow a rule does not confirm that I follow a rule, unless there can be something that will prove my impression correct. And the something cannot be another impression —for this would be 'as if someone were to buy several copies of the morning paper to assure himself that what it said was true' ([*Inv.* I.] 265). The proof that I am following a rule must appeal to something independent of my impression that I am. If in the nature of the case there cannot be such an appeal, then my private language does not have *rules*, for the concept of a rule requires that there be a difference between 'He is following a rule' and 'He is under the impression that he is following a rule' " (*ibid.*).

Castañeda claims that two different arguments are stated in the passage just quoted, one in the first two sentences, the other in the last two. He also claims that a necessary premise has been omitted in both cases. Neither claim, I think, is quite correct. Malcolm is not so much rigorously stating as sketching Wittgenstein's argument in the passage in question, and there is considerable looseness in his presentation of it. I believe the same point is made in the last two sentences quoted as in the first, and the missing premise is clearly implied, if not quite stated. Castañeda, I think, has been over-literal in his reading of Malcolm. If the two pairs of quoted sentences are put together and the implied premise made explicit, Malcolm's argument runs as follows. The proof that someone is following a rule must appeal to something independent of his impression that he is. This something cannot be another impression of his, or anything like an impression—a conviction, an idea, an image, an inclination, or a memory (i.e., a memory-image or memory-belief). The proof must indeed appeal to something outside the subject's mind altogether, something "non-subjective" (cf. *Inv.* I. 265). If in the nature of the case there cannot be such an appeal, then no rule is being followed, and hence no language is being used. Now in the case of the user of a private sign or language, in the case of Privatus or the diary keeper of *Inv.* I. 258, there cannot be such an appeal. Hence a private language is no language, the sign 'E' is no sign, and the use of 'E' is no linguistic activity.

If this is Malcolm's argument (and it seems to me certain that it is), then Castañeda's quarrel with it comes to this: the premise stated in the penultimate step (he would say) "cannot be established." It cannot be established because it is, in his view, false. And it is false because the speaker of a private language "can resort to practically all the 'things' to which the speakers of public, or of ordinary, languages have recourse," "most" of these things being "independent of his impression that he is using a certain word correctly," so that he is able thereby to "correct his mistaken uses of words in essentially the same way in which we normally correct our linguistic errors" (p. 99). What are these "things," and how is Privatus, by "resorting" to them, able to correct his linguistic errors? Castañeda here, unfortunately, is less than clear. He gives several lists and examples of such "things," and of ways in which Privatus can correct himself, but the relation between these various lists is obscure and it is uncertain, often, what a proffered example is supposed to be an example of. There is one list, however, which does appear, with minor variations, three different times (p. 99 twice, p. 101 once), and which appears a fourth time (p. 103) with one item omitted, so I shall take this as canonical and give most of my attention to it.

Five "things" are listed: "Privatus *qua* speaker of Privatish has (i) his experiences and the objects, public or private, which he apprehends in them, (ii) his memories of previous utterances, (iii) the words of Privatish, (iv) the logical connections among these, and (v) the generalizations which link some objects to others" (p. 99, my numbers inserted; earlier on page 99 (iii) is "the noises or marks which constitute our language"). I shall now try to show that, of these five things, (i), (ii) and (iii) are such that recourse to them would in no way prove the correctness of any use of language, much less the use of a private term, and (iv) and (v) are such that recourse to them in order to establish the correctness of the application of a private term is logically ruled out by the very fact that the term in question is private. I shall consider each of these five things, briefly, in turn.

(i) How could an appeal to an "object of our experience" (p. 99), especially a private object, provide a proof of anything? The task would be to prove that my use of a certain word, indeed of a private word, as the name of some private object now present to me is consistent with my past use of the same word; i.e., that I have used this word to refer to and only to objects of the same sort as that to which I am now using it to refer. The object or objects to which I may appeal would also, presumably, be now present to me, either the object to which I am referring or some other. But now if the latter, how would an appeal to it have any bearing on my use of the word in question? The only objects in any way relevant to that, surely, are that present object to which I now refer and those past objects for which I have used the same word. And if the object I appeal to is the object I refer to, it is hard to see how that could prove my use of that referring word for it to be correct. Perhaps I am to scrutinize it very closely, examine it more carefully than I did at first. But I am not sure that the idea of scrutinizing or examining a private object has any sense. And even if it did, what could such scrutiny establish? Something about the object as it revealed itself to my first careless glance led me to use this word for it in the first place. A closer look might convince me that the object really is as I first thought it was, and hence that this is the right word. But that only touches my *conviction*; the question is whether I am *right*, which is to say, whether this *is* the word that I have used for this sort of object in the past. Closer examination of something in the present decides nothing concerning that. Perhaps Castañeda, misled by Malcolm's word 'impression,' has something like this in mind: I have the impression that my use of this word for this object is correct; my impression can be confirmed, its correctness proved, by "having recourse to" the objects of this impression (an impression is an impression *of* something); I check the impression against these objects, determine whether they match, and so on. But this is hopelessly misguided. In the first place, the impression that Malcolm is speaking of is not an impression *of* but an impression *that*, and as such has no object or archetype. Secondly, even if there were an object or archetype, something of which the impression were somehow an image or copy, the notion that I can compare the two is without sense. If I were capable of getting at the object, directly, as it were, there would have been no need—and no room—for the impression in the first place. And if I am not so capable, the best that I can do is compare the original impression with another impression, or something like an impression, be it memory, perception, or whatever, in that it, too, is just an image or copy of the object. This amounts, I think, to a *reductio ad absurdum* of the view that there are such impressions, and in general of what Reid called the idea theory of perception and thought. (I do not say that Castañeda holds this view.)

(ii) What does Castañeda mean by 'memories' in 'memories of previous utterances'? If he means 'memory impressions' or 'memory beliefs' then (ii) reduces to (i), and the same sorts of points made against it apply here as well. If, on the other hand, Castañeda means by 'memories' 'correct memory impressions' —if, i.e., he intends the use of 'memory' which goes with that use of 'remember' whereby 'I remember that p' implies that p—then his saying that Privatus can resort to his memories of previous utterances, and so prove that his present use of language is correct, clearly begs the question. In either case, an appeal to one's memories proves nothing.

(iii) There is an important difference between the words of a language and "the noises or marks which constitute" a language, at least as these expressions are normally understood. Among other things, the former are types, the latter tokens—unless Castañeda does intend the two expressions to be equivalent, in which case I cannot tell which way he means them to be taken. But it really makes no difference, for the result is the same in either case. How is one to appeal to a *word* in a language at all, taking 'word' in the type sense? And even if this could be managed, what would any such appeal prove regarding, say, our diary keeper's use of the sign 'E'? Let us imagine him wondering whether 'E' is the right word for the private object now before his mind, or trying to confirm his impression that it is. It is hard to see how an appeal to any other word of his private language besides 'E' would have any bearing on this question. And it is equally hard to see how an appeal to 'E' would accomplish anything, beyond convincing him that it is the word 'E' that he is now concerned about. Let us suppose, then, that our diary keeper appeals to some noise or mark which "constitutes" a word, i.e., to some token. Again, an appeal to a noise or mark constituting (some utterance or inscription of?) any word other than 'E' would have no relevance to the task at hand. And an appeal to a noise or mark for 'E' would reveal nothing as to the consistency of this present use of 'E' with past uses—which is, after all, what is in question. Besides which, a noise is something heard and a mark something seen, which means that both are objects of experience. Hence the difficulties noted in the discussion of (i) above apply here as well.

(iv) I have been willing to suppose for the sake of argument that Privatish may have "logical terms" as well as private ones, although I actually believe that the Wittgenstein–Malcolm view excludes this. If then there are these logical terms, so will there be "logical connections" among them. But our task is not to prove some application of a *logical* term of Privatish correct; it is the private terms that concern us. The question is, then, whether the private terms of Privatish also exhibit logical connections among themselves and with the logical terms. If so, then I believe it would be possible, in principle, to check the use of a private term by appealing to such logical connections, though the details of how this would be done remain to be worked out. But in fact the private terms of Privatish cannot, I think, be logically related, either to other, non-private terms, or among themselves. For if they were so related, then they would not be private, understandable to no one but their user. This is clearly true in the case of relations to non-private or logical terms. For such terms can be understood by persons other than their user, and this means that another person could deduce and hence understand the meaning of a private term via its logical connections with terms whose meanings are, in principle at least, known to him. The same is true, I think, for the case in which a private term is logically related only to other private terms, although I am not quite clear about this. For it seems to me that a term must have a certain stability, as it were, an established use, in order to sustain logical relations to other terms at all, and such stability is just what is ruled out by the term's being private. Or perhaps "ruled out" is too strong here; perhaps I should say that it is just such stability which is in question in the case of private terms, so that to suppose such a term to have this stability is to beg the question of its being a proper term, or element of language. In any case, an appeal to the logical connections of the private terms of Privatish cannot serve the purpose which Castañeda says it does.

(v) The generalizations to which Castañeda alludes are to "link some objects to others" and they are also to be empirical (pp. 99, 101). I agree that if there were such generalizations linking private objects with non-private or even other private objects, they could be used to prove, or anyhow to make probable, that the use of a certain word for some private object so linked was or was not correct. But how are such generalizations to be established? Presumably, since they are empirical, by observation (or the like) of the objects to be linked. But as I have already indicated, the idea of observing a private object seems to me not to have any sense. More importantly, one can hardly establish or even undertake to establish a general truth about a thing or sort of thing unless one can refer to that thing or sort on different occasions and know that he is referring to the same thing or sort each time. Hence, to establish generalizations about a private object one would have to know that one's intended references to that object were all, or mostly, in fact references to that object; one would have to know, in other words, that one's use of one's private word for that object was consistent. But this knowledge, of course, is just what an appeal to such generalizations is supposed to provide. In short, generalizations about private objects presuppose, and hence cannot provide, the possibility of proving the correctness of references to such objects. And even if the privacy of private objects does not rule out the existence of such generalizations, as I believe it does, it is at least clear that nothing can be proved by them, or nothing to the purpose at hand. I conclude that Castañeda is no more successful with this item than he is with the other four.

I will comment briefly upon a few of the other alleged things by which, or ways in which, Privatus can, according to Castañeda, prove the correctness of his uses of words and correct his linguistic mistakes. Castañeda says that "an English speaker can correct his misapplication of a word simply by noting that the object is not what he called it," and that Privatus can do the same (p. 99). But how is one, or how is Privatus, to "note" any such thing? He has his initial impression that the object is what he called it; is he now supposed to dispense with this impression and grasp the object directly? But if he can do this now, why didn't he do it in the first place? And even if he does get past or go around the impression and get to the object itself, what shows or indeed could show that he "notes" it correctly? Or doesn't this question arise? Castañeda cannot, I think, get any mileage out of this suggestion at all.

On pages 99–100 Castañeda notes that an English speaker who makes a linguistic mistake often "knows of his slip on hearing his utterance of the word [in question], and clearly, both his hearing of it and the noise he hears are independent of his impression that he was using the correct word." "Exactly the same," he then says, "can be said of Privatus." This, I think, is true. But the English speaker knows *on* hearing, not *by* hearing, and certainly not by *his hearing* or by the *noise*, and it is 'by,' not 'on,' that Castañeda needs. How could one know or prove or correct anything *by* his hearing or *by* a noise in any case? Also, the sense in which Privatus' hearing himself speak is *independent* of his impression that he is speaking correctly is not the sense that Malcolm and Wittgenstein intend when they say that a proof must appeal to something independent, as I noted earlier. The noise that Privatus makes may be independent in the required sense, but a noise, surely, cannot be used to prove anything.

Finally, in the case that Castañeda describes on page 100, involving an inference, the following are among the items cited as being "independent of the impression attached to the [speaker's] first use of the word [in question] that it is a correct use": "the desire to make the valid reasoning in question," "the awareness of uttering or thinking that" the major premise of the inference is true, and "the awareness (or 'feeling' or impression) that the validity of the inference requires the two premises to have a common term." Surely, none of these is *either* independent, in the required sense, of the speaker's mind *or* capable of proving the correctness of anything.

I conclude, therefore, that Castañeda fails to make his case against the private-language argument even on his own interpretation of it. He has not shown that a necessary premise of the argument cannot be established. Rather, his own contention that the premise is false has not been established.

Castañeda's case against the private-language argument is unsuccessful, and doubly so. But is the argument then sound? I do not know, but I think this question ought not to be raised until we understand more clearly just what the argument is. Castañeda, I am sure, has not got it right, but knowing this is far from knowing what the correct formulation would be. I will make only one general suggestion on this point. It seems to me that Wittgenstein's essential target in the argument is a certain conception of sensations and feelings, or more generally, the notion of a necessarily private object, one the "possessor" of which alone can possibly know about. Wittgenstein seeks to reduce this notion to absurdity, as I see it, by appealing to linguistic considerations. This of course requires certain premises concerning the relation of language to existence and to knowledge, and concerning the nature of meaning and reference, and hence the argument does throw light upon these subjects. But this, I believe, is incidental to Wittgenstein's main purpose. He is not trying to show something about language but rather about sensations or mental phenomena. Linguistic considerations are the means, but an understanding of the latter is the end. An appreciation of this fact is, I believe, the necessary first step to a full and accurate understanding of the private-language argument.

COMMENTS

JAMES F. THOMSON

It is, as Mr. Castañeda says, widely held that Wittgenstein demonstrated the impossibility of a private language. Castañeda does not share that view. He undertakes to examine the Private-Language Argument as it is sketched, on Wittgenstein's behalf, by Professor Malcolm, and he claims that when the Argument is properly set out it is seen to be either question-begging or inconclusive. Independently of this (if I understand him properly) he thinks that the Argument could not succeed anyway, since its conclusion is false; private languages exist, hence are possible.

I agree with Castañeda that it is not clear at all what the Private-Language Argument is supposed to come to or what its assumptions and its reasoning are. But I think that the difficulties in coming to an understanding of it are much greater than he allows for.

1. Castañeda begins by maintaining that if the notion of a private language is to be given a run for its money, we must be allowed to consider the possibility of "mixed" languages, languages which contain private sub-languages. A language or sub-language is defined to be private if it contains designations for private objects, where these latter are things which satisfy one or more of the conditions on pages 90–91. He now remarks that English contains a private sub-language, since English-speakers talk about their pains and aches and after-images, and these are private objects in one or more of the required senses. He concludes that English is a counter-example to the thesis that a private language is impossible.

Castañeda supposes then that a private language can be taken as one which contains designations for private objects in his, Castañeda's, sense. I do not think it can.

Wittgenstein asks (243) whether there could be "a language in which a person could write down or give vocal expression to his inner experiences—his feelings, moods, and the rest—for his private use." He makes it plain that this language is not to be "our ordinary language," but rather one whose words refer "to what can only be known to the person speaking: to his immediate private sensations." The German here has 'wissen'—"Die Wörter dieser Sprache sollen sich auf das beziehen, wovon nur der Sprechende wissen kann"—so that the idea is that the words of the language are to refer to that about which only the speaker of the language can have knowledge. Wittgenstein adds, "So another person cannot understand the language." The question whether such a language is possible is returned to in 256: "Now what about this language which describes my inner experiences and which only I understand?" Wittgenstein at once makes the point that if there were such a language, a connection would have had to be set up between the words of it and the sensations they stood for. But *how*, he asks, would the connection have been set up? Would it have been set up in the same way as the connection is set up between the English word 'pain' and pain? Then, he replies, the language would not be a private one. For the connection between 'pain' and pain is set up via the natural expression of pain. And because of that, "someone else might understand it [i.e. the language] as well as I."

What then, for Wittgenstein, makes a language not private, is that there is the possibility of its being understood. And that English is a private language in the relevant sense is something quite implausible.

Wittgenstein says that the words of the (hypothetical) private language are to refer to things that only the speaker can know about, and seems to take this to be much the same as saying that they are to refer to his immediate private sensations. Castañeda restates this in terms of designations for private objects. But then he is not at liberty to put his own interpretation on 'private object.' He has a rather easy job making it out that pains are private objects in his sense. But to show that a pain is a private thing in the sense of 243 he would, I think, have to be able to show something like this: if a man has a pain it is possible for him to know something about his pain which it is impossible that anyone else should know. This condition is stronger than any condition to the effect that if a man has a pain then he has a way of getting to know about his pain which it is impossible for anyone else to have. (Compare Castañeda's conditions 2a and 3a for something to be private, and also what he says on page 93 about knowing of a pain privately, apparently just by having it.) It is a stronger condition than is indicated by any of his postulates A through G on page 92, or by J^a. And I conclude that it is also stronger than J^*, since he says that J^* can be derived from A through G. Now that pains are private in this stronger sense is certainly not obvious, nor would Wittgenstein have admitted that it was true (see 246). So I cannot see that Castañeda's counter-example is anything more than an *ignoratio elenchi*.

It is also a surprising one. Castañeda explicitly notices that Wittgenstein infers from his definition of a private language that only its speaker can understand it. It is strange that he never raises the question whether that inference is a correct one. For, of course, if it is, and if English is a partly-private language in the relevant sense, then it seems to follow that someone who says 'I have a toothache' says something which cannot be understood by his dentist or his wife. Does Castañeda accept that conclusion, I wonder?

2. But I now want to make something of the fact that Wittgenstein does not explain or discuss that inference either.

It is usual in this kind of discussion to emphasize that the philosophical question of a private language is of a language which is, as a matter of logical necessity, unintelligible to anyone except its speaker. But this does not by itself explain what the question is. For what would make a language of such a kind that it was logically impossible for anyone but its speaker to understand it? What kind of language is here being envisaged?

Well, as Professor Ayer reminds us,[1] Professor Carnap once held that if a thirsty man says "Thirst now" and is held to be referring to his sensation(s) of thirst, it follows that what he says cannot be understood by his hearers. (Or perhaps it cannot be fully or properly or completely understood.) Carnap concluded that 'Thirst now' does not refer to the speaker's sensation but is rather equivalent to some sentence or set of sentences about his body (Physicalism). Let us try to reconstruct the argument here. Given (A) 'If X says "Thirst now" he says something which if true is made true by his having a sensation of thirst,' and (B) 'No one but X can know whether X has a sensation of thirst,' it does not yet follow that (Z) 'If X says "Thirst now" no one else can understand what he says.' We need some extra premises. It is a reasonable guess that Carnap would have offered something like (C) 'It is possible for Y to understand a sentence only if it is possible for Y to come to know whether the truth-conditions of that sentence are fulfilled.' (C is either a statement of or a consequence of some statement of Verificationism.)

What now about the inference recorded by Wittgenstein in 243, "So another person cannot understand the language"? How is that inference to be explained? Of course we are not now concerned with "our ordinary language," but with some hypothetical language. But we still need to have it explained what is supposed to make that hypothetical language unintelligible to anyone but its speaker. All that we are told is that the words of the language are to refer to the immediate private sensations of the speaker, these being apparently things about which he alone can have knowledge. Perhaps then the operative words here are 'immediate' and 'private.'

[1] A. J. Ayer, "Can There Be Private Language?" in *Belief and Will*, Aristotelian Society, Supplementary Volume XXVIII, London, 1954, pp. 64–65.

And perhaps Wittgenstein would have offered some argument like the one above, but with the word 'sensation' in A and in B replaced by 'immediate private sensation' to yield two statements which we may call A' and B'. But A' and B' do not entail Z. We need still a third premise. Would Wittgenstein have offered Carnap's verificationist premise C? This may be doubted (at any rate it will be denied). But then what third premise are we to supply? For we still need one—for example a premise spelling out the notion of a sensation's being immediate and private.

If we suppose that by the phrase 'immediate private sensations' Wittgenstein means just *sensation*, then the negative side of what Wittgenstein says is barely distinguishable from the negative side of what Carnap says. On this interpretation Wittgenstein would be denying (or would anyway be committed to denying) that we do ever, in any straightforward sense, report on or talk about our sensations at all. (Compare Mr. Strawson's doubts on this very point in *Mind*, 1954.) Their positive suggestions are of course different. Carnap, unwilling to accept Z, rejected A and adopted physicalism. Wittgenstein, on this way of reading him, also rejects Z and therefore A' (which is now the same as A), adopting rather the view that the relevant sentences are to be seen as avowals, pieces of linguistic behaviour which replace certain kinds of unlearned behaviour. I say, 'on this way of reading him,' and of course this way of reading him may be wrong. But the alternative is, I think, that Wittgenstein has no coherent view at all. It is clear that throughout these sections of the *Investigations* he is trying to characterize and expose some way of thinking about sensations, some way which makes them out to be "private objects." It is to this way of thinking about them that he opposes the reminder about how sensation-words are in fact learned, and the connected idea of avowals. But he does not, I think, ever make it clear what is the way of thinking that he wants to expose and discredit. So the alleged disease and the alleged specific pass each other by.

At all events I am inclined to think that the question raised in 243 is obscure. It is obscure because we are not told what is supposed to make the private language a private language. And that surely needs to be explained. For what otherwise can we make of the idea of a private language, a necessarily private language? And, incidentally, if the question whether a private language is possible is an obscure one, mustn't the claim that Wittgenstein answered it be at least as obscure?

3. When Castañeda turns to examine the Private-Language Argument, he proceeds by supposing someone—Privatus—to be speaking or writing a private language, and then asks what objec-

tions can be brought against the consistency of that supposition. He considers some objections which are suggested to him by Malcolm's discussion, and concludes that these objections are either inconclusive or question-begging.

I shall not discuss this part of Castañeda's paper (although I am in agreement with much of what he says). This is because, for one thing, I do not see that there is anything in his supposition about Privatus to make Privatus' language a private one in any interesting sense. But, for another, I think that Castañeda has failed to notice that he and Malcolm are likely to be at cross-purposes.

Malcolm does indeed claim to have sketched a proof by *reductio ad absurdum* that a private language is impossible, in some unexplained sense of 'private language.' But how seriously does Malcolm himself take that claim? Having sketched the line of argument which Castañeda examines, he imagines an objector to say:

"Even if I cannot prove and know that I am correctly following the rules of my private language, . . . still it *may* be that I am. It has *meaning* to say that I am. The supposition that I am makes sense; you and I *understand* it."

Malcolm says that Wittgenstein has a reply to this. The reply consists in likening the sentence 'I am following the rules of my private language' to such sentences as 'The stove is in pain.' These "call up a picture in our minds," and that is about all. So I suppose that if Castañeda were to say, "Even if we cannot prove and know that Privatus is following rules, perhaps all the same he is; the supposition that he is makes sense," then Malcolm's reply would again be the same.

What Malcolm treats as an objection to his view is of course no more (though equally no less) than a rhetorical restatement of the point at issue. So the "reply" to it should consist of or appeal to a complete argument against the possibility of a private language. But it doesn't. It amounts to the *assertion* that the supposition of a private language is not a genuine supposition, or is at least in need of explanation. To be willing to make that reply is not (I would have thought) to be even trying to offer or explain a proof of impossibility. It is rather like offering a challenge: "Make me understand what it would be like for someone to be speaking a private language." It is rather obvious that Castañeda may now issue a challenge of his own: "Make me understand what your difficulty is and that it is a real one."

What future there is for that kind of debate I do not know. But it does seem that Castañeda is writing (not indeed without reason and excuse) as if Malcolm had assumed the burden of proof, and that Malcolm is writing as if the onus of proof or of clarification were on his opponents. If that is so, there is all the more reason for having the terms of the dispute about private languages made clear—or for giving up the whole thing as a mare's nest.

Let me end by stressing the amount of my agreement with Castañeda. (1) It is widely held that Wittgenstein showed something important about the notion of a private language. (2) When we look into this claim, it is not obvious that he did anything of the sort. My disagreement with Castañeda arises over the question whether any clear claim at all has ever been made on Wittgenstein's behalf.

REJOINDERS

H-N. CASTAÑEDA

Concerning Mr. Chappell's comment (A): Although I do not think Mr. Chappell has described in general what a *reductio ad absurdum* properly is, I shall not examine his views thereof. I wish to start with two points which especially need emphasis in the issue between us:

(1) In the reduction of a conjunctive concept P&L to absurdity one can distinguish two cases: (a) there is a concept L' which is a conjunction of only some of the necessary conditions constituting L such that P&L' can also be reduced to absurdity; (b) there is no concept L' as described. In case (a), which seems to be the only one that Chappell allows for, there is, however, *no mistake* in deriving an absurdity directly from P&L. Obviously, since being P&L entails being P&L', if P&L' implies an absurdity, so does P&L. In case (b), the only correct procedure for the reduction is to reduce P&L to absurdity directly. Therefore it is *never* a mistake to spell out *all* the necessary conditions of L when one is trying to reduce some concept P&L to absurdity. Chappell seems not to recognize this.

(2) Let S be a necessary condition for L, and let L* be exactly like L except that L* has S* *instead of* S as a necessary condition. Suppose that P&L* is reduced to absurdity. Clearly, from this alone we cannot correctly infer that P&L can be reduced to absurdity. Furthermore, if the reduction to absurdity depends necessarily on the presence of S* instead of S, then the argument, however conclusive, proves nothing about P&L.

Certainly Wittgenstein is entitled to define 'private language' as he pleases. And if on his definition a private language has no logical words, or only a sign 'E,' I agree that private languages are impossible. But from this it does not immediately follow that private languages are impossible in the sense of *Inv.* I. 243—languages, i.e., whose "individual words refer to what can only be known to the person speaking." Of course, Wittgenstein may conjoin these two features into one definition of private language. But Wittgenstein cannot decide that the possession of one feature entails the possession of the other. Now I claim not to know what Wittgenstein meant to do. But I am anxious to discover whether or not, as Malcolm claims, private languages in the sense of *Inv.* I. 243 are impossible. Clearly, once we have settled on this definition, neither Wittgenstein nor Malcolm has a right, nor do I, to "determine what should and should not be allowed to Privatus" (p. 109) by way of a different definition of private language. Chappell simply overestimates the rights accruing to Wittgenstein and Malcolm in having "introduced the notion of a private language in the first place."

Now if, as Wittgenstein claimed (correctly in my view), a necessary condition for a language is the possession of a systematic structure, then to show that a private language* (i.e., a language deprived of its systematic structure) involves an absurdity is *not* to show that a private language involves an absurdity.

The point is of such importance that I wish to put it over again in another way. Suppose that a language need not have a systematic structure. Then there are two species of private language: (a) one with a systematic structure and (b) one without it. It should be obvious that to show that species (b) *qua* species (b) cannot have instances, is not to show the impossibility of instances of species (a).

I concede that Wittgenstein's suggested arguments are effective to show the absurdity of private languages of certain species: with no logical terms, with only one rule, with only one sign 'E,' etc. But by (1) and (2) above it is a mistake to conclude from this alone that those arguments dispose of the other species, or that there is no other species to consider. And it is of high philosophical importance to determine whether or not another species can have instances—even if Wittgenstein and Malcolm denied them, or never dreamed of them.

Concerning Mr. Chappell's comment (B): By (2), 'Privatish is a private language' is not to be reduced to absurdity by replacing necessary conditions for the existence of a language by conditions which are not necessary. If the having of a criterion for proving that the application of a term of L is correct, is not required for L to be a language, then it is a mistake to object that in a private language there are no criteria for proving that certain applications of its private terms are correct. In accordance with (2), my argument is intended to show either that Privatus while using Privatish has most of the ways of correcting his uses of words available to a speaker of a public language *or else that there is nothing that either speaker has by which he can correct his uses of words*. The latter disjunct is precisely the theme of my insistence on a "fair *reductio*," which insistence did strike Mr. Chappell's attention. Now Mr. Chappell agrees that, say, General Eisenhower knows of his slip in English 'This green . . . I mean red chair . . .' on hearing the word 'green,' just as Privatus could know of a slip involving a private word. But Mr. Chappell stresses that the speaker knows *on* hearing, not *by* hearing, and claims that my argument requires that Privatus corrects himself *by* hearing his word. By (2) this claim is not entirely true. Yet Mr.

Chappell does not consider that Eisenhower also has nothing *by* which to correct himself, if his identification of the color (on a par with Privatus' identification of the properties of his private objects) is not to count as a criterion. Doubtless Mrs. Eisenhower might, correctly, have said: "Not green, but red, Ike." But this is not a criterion *by* which Eisenhower is to correct himself. He has to hear Mrs. Eisenhower's utterance. But the *hearing* of her utterance is not a criterion by which Eisenhower is to correct himself, either. He must understand the utterance; he must understand that it was meant as a correction. And all of this presupposes that he can identify the words of the utterance without criteria; that is, his second-person's or addressee's use of the second-order words 'not,' 'green,' 'but,' 'red,' and 'Ike' *involves no criteria*. Yet this is not enough. Eisenhower must have strong reasons for supposing that Mrs. Eisenhower is right. But the best reasons he can have are only inductive and would *not*, to use Mr. Chappell's term, "prove" that Eisenhower's use of the term 'green' was incorrect. Even if the largest crowd of English speakers joined in saying 'Not green, but red, Ike,' the situation remains unaltered. The choral utterance is not a criterion for Eisenhower; he has both to hear it and to be sure that they have not connived to deceive him, or that each person did not suddenly get an impulse to trick him, etc. There is nothing by which he can *prove* that his utterance of 'green' is incorrect. (If one says that others' correcting utterances function as a criterion because they are *causally* efficient in correcting the speaker of a public language, then one gives up the claim that Privatish fails to be a language in failing to have proofs of correctness or incorrectness. Besides, many different natural events not involving other people may very well cause Privatus to make the necessary linguistic self-corrections to keep up Privatish.)

In regard to Mr. Chappell's paragraph (i): I have only two counter-comments. On the one hand, Mr. Chappell fails to note that most of what he says in (i) applies also to the use of words referring to non-private objects. His conclusion about private language is, by (2), at least over-hasty. On the other hand, Mr. Chappell fails to realize that there is nothing in the characterization of private objects (*Inv*. I. 243) that requires them to be ephemeral and non-coexistent. He argues that Privatus cannot determine whether or not a private object is truly describable e.g. as W on the grounds that the past W's provide no useful comparison, while *the* present object is precisely the one whose W-ness is at issue. This is an incomplete disjunction. Even if we assume that comparisons are required, there is no reason to suppose that Privatus' paradigm of W is not a long-lasting private object steadily present in Privatus' experience with which all objects coexist. For that matter, the paradigm of W can very well be a series of longer-lasting overlapping W's. Thus, Privatus could compare his private (or public) objects with his paradigm of W and determine whether his use of the word 'W' is correct or not. Of course, if paradigms for comparison do not constitute or provide criteria of correctness, they also do not in public languages, thus, by (2), we have here nothing against private languages.

In regard to Mr. Chappell's paragraph (ii): The case of memory is just as difficult for public as for private languages. The point is that without being in a position to *prove* that our memory impressions or judgments are correct or true, we *de facto* get some of them right, and it is this fact, without a proof, which is a necessary condition for the existence of language, public or private.

In regard to his paragraphs (iii) and (iv): As I have argued, we must consider private languages with systematic structure. Thus, (a) some words of Privatish may be definable in terms of others, and (b) some words, though indefinable, have entailment relationships, just as the indefinable 'red' stands, to the term 'extended,' in the entailment relationship exposed by 'Everything red is extended.' In case (a) Privatus can determine whether or not a term or its negation applies to an object; in case (b) he can determine only whether or not one of the two terms applies. Mr. Chappell seems to grant this, but he re-asserts that a term involved in logical relations is not private, i.e., not understandable to the speaker alone. This time he gives a reason: "a term must have stability ... in order to sustain logical relations to other terms at all, and such stability is just what is ruled out by the term's being private ... to suppose a (private) term to have this stability is to beg the question of its being a proper term, or element of language" (p. 116). Now, this reason is not very persuasive; it is difficult to ascertain what a term's stability can be. But even supposing that stability (whatever it may be) is necessary for a term's having logical relations, clearly having no logical relations and referring to private objects are two different concepts. Thus for one thing, he who attacks private languages by claiming that they have no logical terms is precisely *committed* to showing how from the fact that some terms refer to private objects the terms cannot be linked by logical relations; and for another thing, inasmuch as we are reducing 'Privatish is a private *language*' to absurdity, by (1) and (2) above we are not doing anything incorrect and, *a fortiori*, we are begging no question, when we are supposing that Privatish has terms with logical relations, together with whatever this implies, either because all languages must have logical terms, or because though logical terms might not be required yet we choose to consider private languages which do have logical terms.

In regard to (v): Here again Mr. Chappell does not notice that what he says also applies to the case of non-private terms or languages. Yet there is another point. *If* all contingent generalizations are empirical, i.e., accepted by induction, Mr. Chappell would be justified in saying that the use of generalizations in determining the correctness of one's application of a certain word presupposes previous correct applications of the word in question. There should, then, be an independent way, *or else there need be no way in either public or private languages*, of determining the correctness of those previous applications. But here is no problem for Privatish: as remarked in my counter-comments on Mr. Chappell's criticisms (i), (iii) and (iv), either there are no independent criteria in public language any more than in private, or else Privatus may very well have definitions, entailments and paradigms, just as the speaker of a public language has. Clearly, once Privatus holds a generalization in whose acquisition those other means of deciding correctness have been employed, he is in a position to use his generalization in *future* uses of the words entering in its formulation.

But, as Wittgenstein suggested, perhaps not all contingent generalizations are accepted by induction. Perhaps, as he suggested, certain contingent beliefs are required for the possession of a language about certain kinds of objects. Then, if this Kantian-flavored suggestion about language is true, on (1) and (2) above we must allow Privatus the possession of some contingent generalizations without his having come to hold them by induction. This is a very intricate topic, but whatever may ultimately be found to be the case, Mr. Chappell has not shown that I err in allowing Privatus the use of some contingent generalizations.

For Mr. Chappell's commentary, however, I am grateful. He has provided a kind of criticism which has made it possible for me to clarify the point of my arguments more than I could otherwise have hoped to do.

I am pleased to find that Mr. Thomson agrees with my major contentions. For my part I am ready to concede that the obscurities of the private-language argument are much greater than I have allowed for.

1. Mr. Thomson represents me as claiming, *simpliciter*, that private languages exist, that, e.g., our ordinary language of pains is private. My claim, however, is slightly different: that the idea of private language is so obscure that there are many senses of 'privacy' and that in *some* of these senses we find counter-examples. But I am not claiming to have refuted Wittgenstein or Malcolm, for I do not know which sense(s) they had in mind.

2. Next Thomson formulates the condition which in his view is required by *Inv.* I. 293 to make the language of pains a counter-example:

(T) If a man has a pain it is possible for him to know something about his pain which it is impossible that anyone else should know.

Then Thomson argues: "That pains are private in this stronger sense is certainly not obvious, nor would Wittgenstein have admitted that it was true (see 246). *So* I cannot see that Castañeda's counter-example is anything more than an *ignoratio elenchi*" (p. 120, my italics in 'so'). Thomson has, of course, no right to assume that Wittgenstein's refusal to accept that pains are private objects in the relevant sense would be consistent. This is part and parcel of the whole issue. But I want to show that the example of pains is not an *ignoratio*, even in the presence of Thomson's condition (T).

3. There are several senses of 'know' and of 'private object' in which pains have properties that satisfy Thomson's condition (T). Indeed, there is a trivial, obvious property, regardless of the sense of 'know,' which satisfies (T); it is ϕ_1: being a pain had by a person who alone knows that he has the pain. Clearly, it is possible for a man, X, having a pain, to know that he alone knows that he has it; but it is impossible that there is a person different from X who both knows that X has the pain and knows that X alone knows that X has the pain. (Actually, even physical objects may have properties like ϕ_1—e.g., the property of being a rock which X alone knows to be a rock. It is logically impossible that there exist a person Y, different from X, who knows that something is a rock which X alone knows to be a rock. Obviously Wittgenstein did not mean to consider rocks as private objects. Since Thomson's principle (T) is a very natural exegesis of *Inv.* I. 243, this only shows that the idea of private language is so obscure that it defies precise statement.)

Thomson apparently concedes that one knows about one's pains in a way impossible to others. He only contends that this is not enough to yield a counter-example since it does not amount to (T). Let us write 'X KNOWS that P' to indicate that X has knowledge in the unique, first-person way, that P. Consider now the property ϕ_2: being X's pain such that whoever knows that X has it KNOWS that X has it. Here ϕ_2 satisfies (T). Clearly, it is possible for X to know about his pain p that he has p and that every man who knows this KNOWS it—for instance, in one possible case, because he knows that he is the only man in the universe. But if a man Z, different from X, knows that X has p then he knows this in the third-person or second-person way; thus, it is not the case that Z KNOWS that X has p. But then Z cannot know that every man, including himself, who knows that X has p KNOWS that X has

p. Therefore, for every man X and every pain p that X has, it is possible for X to know that p has ϕ_2 while it is impossible that anyone else knows that p has ϕ_2. (The proof requires the obvious principles that "X knows that P" entails P and that "X knows that P and Q" entails "X knows that P and X knows that Q".)

4. Thomson may rejoin that it is only a contingent matter whether a certain pain has either the property ϕ_1 or the property ϕ_2. Hence, it is not necessary that all pains be private objects in the sense of having ϕ_1 or ϕ_2. This is all true, provided that we read *Inv.* I. 243, not as requiring merely Thomson's (T), but also the following:

(T'). If a man has a pain, then *there is something about the pain* which it is possible for him to know and which it is impossible for anybody else to know.

I agree that not all pains have ϕ_1 or ϕ_2. Furthermore wherever a pain has ϕ_1 or ϕ_2, it does not have it necessarily. Thus, it is *possible* that no pain is in fact a private object in the sense of meeting condition (T'), so far as ϕ_1 or ϕ_2 is concerned. But this is enough for my purpose. Wittgenstein's thesis is supposed to be that private languages are impossible; hence that our language of pains is necessarily not about private objects. But if pains may be private objects, even if in fact they are not, then it is certainly false that our language of pains is necessarily not private, even if in fact it is not.

Note, incidentally, that neither (T) nor (T') requires that one knows that one's own pains are private objects, i.e., that one knows that one alone knows that they have (or may have) the property which nobody else can know that they have (or may have). Thus, for all we know many of our pains, in particular our unexpressed and unmentioned pains, may (as is quite likely) have had property ϕ_2, namely, of being known only by those who have KNOWN them, even though we have failed to know this in turn. Thus, it is likely that our language of pains is in fact at least a mixed language, since at least *some* pains are probably private as required by the strong principle (T'), even though we are unable to tell which ones are private.

5. Matters are not so clear as Thomson suggests. There are senses of 'know' in which one knows only what one has *conclusively* verified. And in such senses, all pains are private objects even in the sense indicated by (T'). And there are yet weaker senses of 'know' in which others may know that one is in pain, but not that one's pains present *to one* a certain quale with a certain degree of intensity. Thus, either the following property ϕ_3 or its negation will make pains private objects in the sense indicated by (T'): being

a pain felt by X and having the same quale and intensity as a previous or later pain felt by X. Doubtless, X himself may fail to know that a given pain of his has (or lacks) ϕ_3. But this is irrelevant. Neither (T) nor (T') requires that X knows that his pains are private objects.

6. Thomson reinforces his charge of *ignoratio* by asking whether I accept that a dentist cannot understand his patient's 'I have a toothache.' But Thomson does not mention that 'understand' is as unclear as 'know.' Here the dentist does not understand fully the patient's utterance of 'toothache' to the extent that he fails to know the thing the patient is referring to. Once again, if knowing the thing referred to requires acquaintance with or experience of it, then if the postulate of privacy is a necessary truth, the dentist does not understand the utterance fully. If knowing the thing referred to requires complete personal verification that the patient has it, then even if the privacy postulate is false, the dentist does not understand fully. And so on through my list of senses of 'private object.'

7. Thomson is somewhat unfair to the defenders of the private-language argument. I do find in their writings arguments which do more than beg the question. Some of the arguments do prove that certain kinds of language are impossible, e.g., a language with only words referring to private objects or with no logical terms. Unfortunately some of their arguments also prove too much: they require conditions which are not met by ordinary languages, or even that part of existing languages which is just about material objects.

8. In conclusion, I am content with claiming simply that I have refuted the private-language argument in all its forms, so that concerning the private-language issue there is simply an impasse. I have some doubts about the possibility of settling the matter conclusively either way. But I think that further careful examination of the issue and arguments is required, in spite of there being a "mare's nest." In philosophy we ought to work carefully to erect impasses, to build philosophical views on each side of the impasse, and examine the views on their over-all merits; then we may find a solution for the impasse. Thus, while I find valuable the efforts of Malcolm and other Wittgensteinians at building views on the assumption that private languages are impossible, I feel that with Thomson's support, I have earned a right to philosophize on the assumption that private languages *are* possible. I am glad that Thomson has helped me to make this clearer.

www.ingramcontent.com/pod-product-compliance
Lightning Source LLC
Chambersburg PA
CBHW020656300426
44112CB00007B/407